DOROTHY JEWSON

Further details of Poppyland Publishing titles can be found at
www.poppyland.co.uk
*where clicking on the 'Support and Resources' button
will lead to pages specially compiled to support this book*

Join us for more Norfolk and Suffolk stories and background at
www.facebook.com/poppylandpublishing

'Justice Demands The Vote': suffragette poster.

Dorothy Jewson

Suffragette and Socialist

by

Frank Meeres

Copyright © 2014 Frank Meeres

First published 2014 by Poppyland Publishing, Cromer, NR27 9AN
www.poppyland.co.uk

ISBN 978 1 909796 04 1

All rights reserved. No part of this publication may be reproduced, stored in a retrieval system or transmitted by any means, mechanical, photocopying, recording or otherwise, without the written permission of the publishers.

Designed and typeset in 10.5 on 13.5 pt Gilgamesh by Watermark, NR27 9ER
Printed by Lightning Source

Picture credits
Images are reproduced by courtesy of the following:
Archant (*Eastern Daily Press*): pages 20, 24, 49, 50, 62 (top), 68, 72, 73, 77, 78
Michael Jordan: 19
London Metropolitan University (TUC Library Collections): 41
Norfolk Record Office: 2, 10 [BR 35/4/34], 26 [Y/TPL 3/2], 40 [FC 10/18], 43 (bottom) [MC 655/44], 44 [MC 43/130], 47 [MC 2183], 51 (top) [MC 2956], 62 (bottom) [MC 43/103], 83 [N/LM 2/8], 85 and 88 [both MC 2959], 92 [MC 43/130]
Norwich High School for Girls: 11, 12, 13
People's History Museum, Manchester: 51 (bottom)

Contents

1	Early life and career	7
2	The suffrage movement in Norwich	16
3	'The Destitute of Norwich and How they Live'	27
4	Dorothy Jewson as pacifist and union worker: 1914–22	35
5	The 1923 General Election in Norwich	48
6	Dorothy in Parliament: 1923–24	55
7	Leading from the left: 1924–37	66
8	Dorothy and local politics: 1927–37	82
9	Afterwards: 1937–64	91
Notes		95
Index		98

The Jewson dynasty: Dorothy's father, George on the right.

I
Early life and career

Dorothy Jewson was born on 17 August 1884.[1] She was the daughter of George and Mary Jewson of *Braemar*, a large house off the Thorpe Road on the eastern side of Norwich. George was the eldest son of a family of twelve – eight sons and four daughters – all

Braemar, Cotman Road, Thorpe Hamlet, Norwich: Dorothy was born in this house.

of whom survived childhood, giving Dorothy no shortage of aunts and uncles. He made his fortune as head of the Jewson timber firm, which had begun in Earith, Huntingdonshire, where he was born. It expanded to Norwich in 1868 when George's father, John Wilson Jewson, bought the property later known as 18–20 Colegate; it had a river frontage and two fine eighteenth-century houses, still there today. It cost the substantial sum of £1,000. John Wilson Jewson died in 1882. He had lived in the Colegate property; after his death it was used entirely as offices and the family lived in Thorpe.

Two views of the Jewsons' timber yard in Norwich, between Colegate and the river.

EARLY LIFE AND CAREER

George was a member of the National Liberal Club and had worked for the election of local Liberal MPs like Jacob Henry Tillett and George White. He took public service seriously, serving on the Norwich Board of Guardians from 1882 and becoming a city alderman in 1895. He was also a Justice of the Peace. He was Chairman of the Yarmouth Port and Haven Commissioners from 1904 and was a trustee of the Great Hospital in Norwich. In 1874 he married Mary Jarrold of Norwich.

Mary was well connected too: she was the daughter of Samuel Jarrold and his wife Mary, part of the well-known Norwich family who ran Jarrold's department store in the city. Jarrold's were printers and publishers too, most famously publishing Anna Sewell's classic story *Black Beauty*. She served on the Committee of the Orphans' Home in Norwich which had been founded in 1845, and which was in Chapelfield from 1870. She was a member of St Mary's Baptist Church in Norwich for over 50 years, and ran an adult school at the Chapel.

Dorothy was herself a member of a large family: the Jewsons had eight children, of whom she was the fifth. Three of her siblings died in infancy or childhood — even the rich were not immune from the terrors of child mortality in the late nineteenth century. The eldest child was William Henry, always known as Harry, born in 1875 and nine years old when Dorothy was born. Two sisters, Edith and Ellen Margaret (known as Margaret), were six and seven years older than Dorothy; Edith was to go on to Holloway College in London. Another son, George — always known as Jack — had been born in 1880 but died eight months before Dorothy was born. Dorothy was followed by Clifford, born the year after her; he died in 1898 at the age of twelve. Next came Kathleen, born in 1887: she died in Stuttgart, Germany, in 1905, aged seventeen. The youngest child was John Christopher, always known as Christopher, who was born when Dorothy was six years old. Harry and Christopher were the two to play the greatest parts in Dorothy's story.

Dorothy was educated at Norwich High School for Girls, which was then in the Assembly House in the centre of the city. This school had been founded in 1875 by the Girls' Public Day School Company

The Assembly Rooms, Norwich, formerly Norwich High School for Girls, where Dorothy went to school.

(now Girls' Day School Trust), and was their first school outside London. The school aimed to supply girls with 'a really good education at moderate cost'. An article in a school magazine in 1892 summed up the ambition of the school:

> *The girl of today is not a weak, flabby kind of creature, capable of nothing but classics and mathematics. She must be able to beat her brother at cricket and tennis, and if she cannot skate, row, swim, play hockey and golf and cycle, she is rather a poor sort . . . The modern girl must have a soul that soars above this and be able to discuss politics, the last new book author, and play with perfect freedom, intelligence and understanding. A knowledge of the state of affairs in every empire, kingdom and republic under Heaven . . . is also indispensable.*[2]

Dorothy began at the school in 1891, when she was seven. She was there for over eleven years, leaving in July 1903. The headmistress throughout all her time there was Miss Elizabeth Gadesden who became headmistress in 1884, retiring only in 1907. When Dorothy was in her teens, some time after 1901, the family moved into an even grander house, Tower House in Bracondale, Norwich, named after the medieval tower to which it is attached. They also owned a country retreat at Gimingham, on the north-east coast of Norfolk.[3]

Some of Dorothy's first public appearances can be found within the pages of the school magazine. She played a starring role at the Tennis Club dance, held on 21 November 1901: she was one of four girls asked to do the 'skirt dance'. The girls 'who all luckily had on their accordion pleated frocks, danced some graceful steps, while everyone else sat round the

Tower House, Bracondale, Norwich: the Jewsons moved here when Dorothy was a teenager.

EARLY LIFE AND CAREER

School photograph of about 1896. Left to right are: STANDING: *L. Bignold, M. Campbell, E. Barton, — Arnold, Dorothy's cousin Constance Jewson, Millicent H. Roche;* SEATED: *M. Beverley, E. Jacob, K. Hotblack, — Griffith, Miss Barrett, H. Burton, O. Jarvis, Dorothy Jewson.*

room'. The skirt dance ended with each girl making a pirouette and sinking to the ground with their skirt spread out; 'the performance was enthusiastically applauded' — perhaps Dorothy's first opportunity to impress an audience.

She was a sporty girl, being one of the school's two 'champions of tennis' in

The school team in 1899: Dorothy is second from the left in the back row, Connie holds the trophy.

DOROTHY JEWSON

Dorothy captains the hockey team, 1902. Left to right, BACK ROW: *cousin Daisy Jewson, A. C. P. Lunn, cousin Connie Jewson, unknown, Millicent H. Roche, Dora Arnell, M. Bolingbroke;* FRONT ROW: *sister Kathleen Jewson, unknown, Dorothy Jewson, Ethel Read, Daisy Osborne.*

1902, and playing for the hockey team. She shot three goals when the school beat Thetford High School on 30 November 1901. In March 1902 the school played against Blackheath and, as Dorothy was now team captain, she had to make a speech afterwards: she noted that both schools had a head teacher with the uncommon name of Gadesden [they were actually sisters] and declared that 'if she could not have been a pupil at Norwich school, she would most desire to be a Blackheath one' – she had already learnt how to win over an audience!

She was very bright, too, especially at Latin: she was one of three girls given special mention in this subject when she was in the sixth form, and in unprepared translation she was top of the class 'having translated this passage more faultlessly than any girl who has taken the paper'. She was one of two girls in the school to pass the entrance examination for Girton College in Cambridge in 1903. In September, when she was nineteen years old, Dorothy went to Cheltenham Ladies' College to prepare for the Cambridge Higher Local exam. In fact she did not take this exam but in September 1904 went on to Girton College, where she studied classics and gained a BA. The college that became Girton had been established in 1869 as Britain's first residential college for women: originally in Hitchin, it moved to Girton near Cambridge in 1873. By 1902 the college accommodated 180 students. Dorothy took the classics tripos: she obtained her BA degree in 1907 (technically from Trinity College, Dublin: the

Dorothy in her final year at school. Left to right are: Dorothy Jewson, M. Campbell, D. Denham, H. Gould, M. Beverley.

University of Cambridge was not yet ready to offer degrees to women!). She went on to Cambridge Training College and obtained her Teachers' certificate the following summer.[4]

Dorothy was in fact the kind of bright girl about which her cousin Percy Jewson wrote a barbed verse in 1905:

> *Early we rise, and long we read,*
> *(Every hour of the day indeed)*
> *German and History, Science and French!*
> *Nothing our ardour for learning can quench.*
> *Anxiously thinking of 'trips' to come*
> *(With first-class honours, we hope for some)*
> *When by our achievements all folks may see*
> *How superior women to men must be.*[5]

It was at Girton that Dorothy came under the thrall of the two ideas that were to give purpose to her whole life: Socialism and Feminism. The background to each needs a little explanation.

The Labour Party grew out of three different groups of people dedicated to the **Socialist** cause. The first was the *Social Democratic Federation*. This was founded in 1881, with the object of promoting a Parliamentary Labour Party. The second group was the *Fabian Society*, founded in 1884. It mainly consisted of intellectuals like Sidney and Beatrice Webb, H. G. Wells and George Bernard Shaw. Their aim was not to establish an independent political party, but to spread their influence within the Liberal Party.

The third group was the *Independent Labour Party* founded by Keir Hardie in 1893 with the single aim of getting members of the working class into Parliament. Unlike the other two groups, the Independent Labour Party was committed to winning the support of trade unions to the cause. The next step forward came in 1900. Delegates from the ILP, the SDF and the Fabian Society met together with delegates representing over half a million trades unionists. They set up the *Labour Representation Committee*, with James Ramsay MacDonald of the ILP as its secretary. However, all three continued as separate organisations. Dorothy joined the Fabian Society when she was at Girton, but very soon moved into the Independent Labour Party, to which she remained loyal throughout her political life.

There had been some activity in direction of **women's suffrage** in the nineteenth century with the formation of several groups promoting the cause. A decisive step forward came when the *National Union of Women's Suffrage Societies* (NUWSS) was founded in 1897 by Millicent Fawcett: its members were known as *suffragists*. Dorothy's mother, Mary, and her aunt, Henrietta Jewson, were both members of this group. A rival group, the *Women's Social and Political Union* (WSPU), was founded in 1903 by Emmeline Pankhurst and her daughters Christabel and Sylvia: they thought the already-existing group was insufficiently dynamic, and also too middle class. It was this group that Dorothy was to join. They were a militant group, but this word needs to be placed in the context of its time. The militant acts of the later twentieth century are a world apart from the militancy of the suffragettes. Their 'militancy' consisted at first of shouting down politicians, and of marches which often involved confrontation with the police. In 1905 Christabel Pankhurst and Annie Kenney attacked a policeman who tried to remove them after they interrupted a meeting held by Sir Edward Grey. They were fined and, on refusing to pay, were sent to prison. From this time the members of the WSPU became known as *suffragettes*, a title of which Dorothy was later to be proud.

Girton College naturally was a force in the struggle to obtain the vote for women. There was a college suffrage society by 1907, and in 1909, by which time it had become part of the Cambridge University Woman's Suffrage Society, there were 97 members from Girton — including all the members of staff! By this time, however, Dorothy had left to take up work.

In 1908, Dorothy became a schoolteacher at a girls' boarding school, West Heath School, Ham Common, Kingston in Surrey. The school had opened in 1865, founded by Revd Philip Power and his wife, Emma, moving to Ham in 1879, where it occupied a large house formerly owned by the Duc de Chartres. (It later moved to Sevenoaks where Diana, Princess of Wales, and her sisters were pupils. The Ham building is now the Cassel Hospital.) The school was purchased by Emma Lawrence and Margaret Skeat in 1900. These two spinsters acted as co-principals of the school and it was they who appointed Dorothy: she was one of six assistant live-in teachers. The girls were of eleven years and upwards, and came from all over the country and occasionally from further afield.

Dorothy was still in Ham in April 1911. Later in the year she moved back to Norwich and lived once more with her parents at Tower House, Bracondale. She apparently took up a position in a former Board School in Norwich, or so she later claimed. I have not been able to find her name in any school records of the time, nor is her name to be found among the teachers paid by the City Council: perhaps she worked in a voluntary capacity. Alternatively, she might have worked in a school outside the city boundary, Trowse being the most likely as it is within walking distance of her Bracondale home; unfortunately staff records of the County Council, which would be her employer here, have not survived. In a speech during her 1923 election campaign she said she had been employed in union activities since 1911, so she probably began work for the National Union of Teachers at the same time.

At this stage in her career Dorothy was working for women's suffrage rather than for socialism, 'believing the former to be an essential step to the latter'. She joined the WSPU on her return to Norwich in 1911, when the local branch was founded.[6]

2

The suffrage movement in Norwich

It was the charisma of the Pankhursts that attracted younger women into the WSPU rather than the NUWSS. In 1910 Christabel Pankhurst spoke at Great Yarmouth, creating an impression that 21-year old Henrietta Grenville was to remember over 60 years later: 'I was so impressed by her elegance, the way she put things. I was convinced by what she had to say and after hearing her, wrote to headquarters to ask what I could do'.[7]

The WSPU had adopted a programme of increasing 'violence', including breaking the windows of government buildings from 1908, hunger strikes from 1909 and attempts to burn down buildings from 1913. However this violence was always aimed against property, *never* against people. Every act of arson by the WSPU was carefully planned by the organisation who were determined that 'not a cat, dog or canary' would be harmed. This was faithfully carried out: the only people ever harmed were the suffragettes themselves. By no means all members of the WSPU were in favour of even this amount of aggression, and several members resigned in protest.

The WSPU came to Norwich in 1911: previously East Anglia had been run through the Ipswich office, with Grace Roe as the area organiser. Margaret West was the first organiser in Norwich, and Dorothy one of the branch's founder members. In April 1912 an office was opened at 52 London Street, with Miss Harmer and Rosa Howlett as local secretaries. A public meeting was held at the Thatched Assembly Rooms in May 1912, with Jane Brailsford, one of the leading speakers in the WSPU, as the main speaker.

Suffragette meeting at Norwich Hippodrome: these are members of the NUWSS, which several of Dorothy's relatives supported.

Dorothy's brother Harry was also a supporter, often putting up the money for the hire of halls. When the WSPU held a big meeting on Norwich Market Place on Sunday 28 July 1912, Harry presided at one of the two platforms. Speakers included local figures like Annie Reeves and one national figure, Leonora Tyson: Jane Brailsford had intended to speak, but problems with the London Underground prevented her. Annie said: 'we are tired of men thinking us angels. We want them to think us women'. Leonora commented that women had decided 'that the men of this country are not even reasonable animals, because if they were led by reason we should have had the vote long ago'. The *Suffragette* magazine listed a Miss Jewson as contributing to the success of the meeting, which was attended by more than 2,000 people. Although several members of the Jewson family worked in campaigns towards women's suffrage, the only one who could be so described at a WSPU meeting is Dorothy, who thus enters the suffragette arena for the first time.

The WSPU in Norwich invited Emmeline Pankhurst herself to speak at a meeting at St Andrew's Hall, Norwich, on 11 December 1912. The front seats cost a shilling, the seats in the middle sixpence and those nearer the back were just two pence. During the day several post-boxes in Norwich had had burning rags pushed into them. This was a common WSPU tactic, but Margaret West denied that they were involved, claiming that it was part of a plot to incite the people of Norwich to create a disturbance at the meeting.

By 7.30 pm, the Hall was packed out, mainly with young men in the cheap seats looking for trouble. Their aim was to prevent Mrs Pankhurst from speaking and the men were armed with whistles, mouth-organs and penny-shriekers of various kinds. When tired of shouting, the mob stamped in unison or sang popular songs of the day. 'We All Go the Same Way Home' and 'Are We Downhearted?' were sung dozens of times. Another popular chorus was 'On the Ball, City', one of the earliest documented uses of this popular local football chant. Mrs Pankhurst remained calm and made her speech, but it was almost inaudible even to those just a few feet from her.

This was Mrs Pankhurst's first visit to Norwich. She was philosophical about it, saying: 'After all it is not the object in my life to obtain a hearing in Norwich. My object is to get women's suffrage, and it is immaterial to me whether or not a number of young men choose to interrupt proceedings.'

The disturbance actually helped attract support for the suffragette cause from some people. A local doctor, Shephard Taylor, wrote to the press: 'When a suffragette takes it upon herself to interrupt a meeting at which Lloyd George or Asquith is making a political speech, she runs a serious risk of being dragged out of the hall by the hair of her head or of being thrown unceremoniously through a window, whereas when a body of roughs attempt to howl down a suffragette speaker, they are left severely alone to carry out their own sweet will and pleasure, while the policemen look on complacently and enjoy the sport with the rest of the company'.

'A mere man' wrote: 'the large majority of the meeting yesterday would gladly have heard Mrs Pankhurst. They were disappointed; but they bought pamphlets by the score. Financially the meeting was a huge success. The interest aroused will not die down, but will be kept alive by further militant tactics if necessary until they are stopped – by the vote'. *The Suffragette* carried a short report of the incident in Norwich, claiming that although Mrs Pankhurst was not heard by the main audience, she was able to turn her back and give an address to 300 'working women' who were sitting in the gallery behind the podium.

On 5 December there was a reception at the Thatched Assembly Rooms. The main speakers were local WSPU campaigners Kathleen Jarvis and Winifred Mayo. However, fun was on the menu too: Dorothy and Olive Jarvis provided the entertainment, a duologue called 'A Chat with Mrs Chicky': this, said the *Suffragette*, 'was very much appreciated'.

On 21 January 1913, George Lansbury held a rally at the Agricultural Hall in Norwich. The first speaker was one of the WSPU leaders, Georgina Brackenbury.

Saint Andrew's Hall, Norwich, where Emmeline Pankhurst spoke in December 1912.

She referred back to the Pankhurst debacle:

> *Mrs Pankhurst would far rather have seen that gathering of excitable and hysterical men as she did the other day – she would far rather have seen the Norwich men getting purple in the face with excitement over that question than to have found empty benches and nobody paying any attention to what was said.*

Two days after Lansbury's speech in Norwich a group of working women met the Liberal leaders Lloyd George and Edward Grey in London. They included about twenty from Norwich. However, on the same day as this meeting the Speaker announced that he had decided it was not possible to add clauses allowing women's franchise to the Franchise Bill currently being considered in Parliament: a totally new bill would have to be drawn up. In practice, this meant that there would be no women's suffrage in the immediate future. The truce was over. Mrs Pankhurst declared: 'we will fight for the vote as Garibaldi fought for Italian freedom'. At a meeting held at this time she said 'it is guerrilla warfare that we declare this afternoon'.[8]

At first, the campaign in Norwich continued as before, with meetings and jumble sales. As well as supporting Lansbury, Georgina Brackenbury gave a speech at the Thatched Assembly Rooms: 'thanks to Mr [Harry] Jewson for lending Hall for meeting and providing teas for 180 women'. This meeting was presumably attended by the middle and upper class supporters of the cause. According to the *Suffragette*,

Georgina also addressed 'two large and enthusiastic groups of working women'.⁹

Dorothy was one of about 20 women thanked in the same paper in February 1913 for her help in organising jumble sales and a stall in Norwich Market Place: others included Mrs Witard and Miss Pratt, names that will recur in this book. 'Mrs Witard' was Agnes, the wife of Herbert Witard, the first ILP man on Norwich City Council. Miriam Pratt was a friend of Dorothy and her brother. She had been born in Surrey in 1890, but was brought up in Norwich by her uncle, a local policeman. She had begun her career as a pupil teacher at Nelson Street School. She moved to Sir George White School for Girls in September 1907: her address at this date was 1 Mill Hill Road. She left the school at the end of August 1908 to attend Homerton College in Cambridge. She returned in 1911 to become a teacher at St Paul's school in Norwich – and, as we shall see, became an active and militant suffragette.[10]

The campaign against property was fought hard in Norfolk. On the morning of Sunday 6 April 1913 a mansion at Eaton Chase, off Newmarket Road in Norwich, was found to be ablaze. The house had been built for W. H. Webster, but he had died suddenly and the interior of the house was unfinished. Suffragettes were suspected. Margaret West was non-committal. She said that she neither claimed nor disclaimed responsibility – 'in view of what was happening in other parts

Eaton Chase, Norwich – destroyed by suffragettes.

Buntings in Norwich, subject of a suffragette attack.

of the country it might well be the work of suffragettes'. *The Suffragette* reported the Eaton Chase fire in the same way as it did other arson attacks, with relish but without actually stating that it was started by suffragettes.

Damage to shop-fronts, another suffragette activity, also came to Norwich. In May 1913 the words 'Votes For Women' were found cut, in seven-inch high letters, into all the plate-glass windows of Bunting's drapery store just before the shop was due to be formally opened. The opening had to be postponed and the glass replaced.

Even while she had been working for women's suffrage in 1912–13, Dorothy had been campaigning for the poor in Norwich; this is considered in the next chapter.

In May the attention of the Norwich branch of the WSPU switched to Cambridge, where a by-election was being held. On 18 May two buildings were burned down in the town, first a new house being built for a Mrs Spencer of Castle Street, then a new genetics laboratory. Suffragette leaflets were found in both. A lady's gold watch was discovered outside the window of the laboratory which had been broken to get in. On 22 May Miriam Pratt was remanded for a week, bail being refused. She was aged 23 and of 9 Turner Road Norwich. Police Sergeant Ward said Miriam was his niece and lived with him and his wife. He had given her a watch about five years earlier. He had read about the Cambridge incident, and remembering that Miriam had recently lost his watch, asked if it was hers. She denied it at first, but eventually admitted to him that she had been at Cambridge with two other people. She had a wound on her hand: she had cut it while trying to scrape out the putty round the window with her scissors. She begged him not to tell anyone but he 'shopped' her anyway.

Her uncle said that Miriam paid him ten shillings a week in rent. She sold suffragette newspapers in the street and had keys to the suffragette offices in London Street. According to him she had been at college in London for two years. Miriam was remanded in prison for eight days. She appeared at the court on 30 May 'with a smile of greeting for some of the ladies in court. She was wearing a blue dress and white gloves, and had a posy of sweet peas at her breast'. Bail was agreed with two sureties of £200 each: Harry Jewson put up one and an unidentified Cambridge lady the other.[11]

The case swept up the other Norwich suffragettes. Margaret West had been in Cambridge with Miriam, helping run the WSPU campaign in the East Cambridgeshire by-election. She was present in court. Dorothy was closely involved too: she organised Miriam's defence fund. The trial was not to be held for a further four months: in the meantime Miriam was suspended from her teaching work at St Paul's school; the Education Committee in Norwich instead employed her in their central office, pending her trial.[12]

The local campaign continued through these summer months of 1913. In June the Norwich group announced that they would hold countryside meetings: 'will those who can cycle and are willing to help work up the Meetings send in their names' to organiser Margaret West. The branch also went to the coast to try and win over holidaymakers to the cause. However, these local happenings were soon overshadowed by a national tragedy.

Perhaps the most sensational single event in the suffragette campaign occurred on 4 June 1913. Emily Davison, a member of the WSPU, bought a third class ticket to Epsom. She stood at Tattenham Corner to watch the Derby. As the king's horse approached, she ran onto the course and grabbed its bridle. The horse rolled over her injuring her severely. She lingered for several days, dying at 4.30 pm on 8 June.

Her death naturally filled the newspapers for days, giving enormous publicity for the cause. It caused ripples locally too: on 13 June there was a meeting of the Norwich WSPU at the Thatched Assembly Rooms, chaired by Margaret West. The main speaker was Marie Naylor from London. She said that critics of the movement had described it as being made up of silly hysterical girls, led by a few clever women: they were entirely ignorant of the type of women who belonged to it.

Emily's funeral took place on the following day. Her coffin was carried across London at the head of an enormous procession of women. They processed to King's Cross station, where the coffin was put onto a train to Morpeth, Northumberland, Emily's home town, for burial. The Norwich WSPU sent a wreath to Davison's funeral with a text that read:

> THE LOVE OF LIBERTY WITH LIFE IS GIVEN;
> AND LIFE THE INFERIOR GIFT OF HEAVEN.

This is a quotation from a Dryden poem in which two knight suitors outdo each other to impress a princess — whose name just happens to be Emily. This high level of literary awareness probably came from Dorothy — and it was almost certainly too high-brow for most of the onlookers!

Several suffragette women chose to go on hunger strike in protest at their conditions. This led to the horrors of forcible feeding, an unbelievably painful and humiliating process which outraged many people who were otherwise indifferent to the cause. However, the alternative was to let the women die, which would have created martyrs. The Home Secretary, Reginald McKenna, came up with an idea to get around the problem. He rushed through an Act in March 1913 which provided that a hunger striker would be released if her life was in danger but would have to go back to prison as soon as she was well enough to do so. This became known as the Cat and Mouse Act.

On 3 July, Clara Giveen and Kitty Marion were convicted of setting fire to the Grandstand at Hurst Park racecourse on the night of 8 June, the day of Emily Davison's death. Clara said that no sentence should be passed as they had not been convicted by a jury of their peers: 'until women were on the jury as well as men no sentences should be passed upon women'. The women were both sentenced to three years imprisonment. Both went on hunger strike and were released within a week under the new Act.

Some years earlier Clara had worked with Margaret West in the WSPU offices in London Street in Norwich, so that she was known to the Norfolk suffragettes. Margaret West wrote to the *Eastern Daily Press* on Friday 18 July, announcing a protest meeting on the Sunday. On Saturday a letter appeared over the names of Dorothea Jewson, Fred Henderson, the Socialist writer and city councillor Herbert Witard, and two Norfolk clergymen, W. H. Marcon and Anthony Fenn. It urged people to attend the meeting against the Cat and Mouse Act:

> *Under it women are just as assuredly — if more slowly and less dramatically — being killed, as they were under the old barbarous system of forcible feeding.*

The letter concluded 'We wish it to be understood that support of the meeting does not in any way involve support of militant methods'. The protest meeting was held in Norwich Market Place on 20 July. The speakers included Henderson, Margaret West and Kathleen Jarvis; some 2,000 people attended. Miriam Pratt was also there; no doubt she was thinking ahead to her own likely imprisonment. A photograph of her at the meeting was published in the local newspaper, which drew her continued suffragette activities to the notice of her employers. A meeting of the Norwich School Staff Committee on 15 September voted (by five votes to one) that her salary would only be paid if 'she absolutely refrained from taking part in any public demonstration with that Movement'.[13]

On 14 October Miriam's trial was held at last. She conducted her own defence and skilfully cast doubt on the evidence of the watch. She said that it was a very plain one, implying that it might have belonged to anyone. Her final statement, however, was not a summing up of her case but a plea for a redress of the wrongs of women:

Meeting in the Norwich Market Place 1913 – the lady in the large hat is Miriam Pratt.

> *I, as a teacher, am in a position to appreciate to the full the unfair distinction made between men and women teachers. In every one of our great cities and in most of our towns there are thousands of wretched women living in conditions of unspeakable filth and horror, who, by working day and night, and with the assistance of their children, even the babies, cannot earn six shillings, five shillings, even three shillings or two shillings a week.*

At one point the judge interrupted her long speech to ask what it had to do with the case. When she replied that she was making her defence he retorted 'I thought your defence was that you did not do it (Laughter)'. The all-male jury seem to have been in sympathy with the judge rather than the accused: they were only out for five minutes before returning with a verdict of guilty.[14]

In fact the arson attempt had been put together by Olive Bartels, the WSPU organiser in Cambridge, who had chosen the target and bought and supplied the paraffin used, but there is no doubt that it was Miriam who did the actual deed. She was sentenced to eighteen months in prison; naturally, she was also dismissed from her teaching post. Miriam immediately went on hunger strike and was transferred to Holloway. She was very soon released for seven days under the Cat and Mouse Act, and went to recover with friends in Kensington.[15]

On the Sunday after Miriam's conviction, Dorothy and other local suffragettes organised a protest at Norwich Cathedral, where the judge who had sentenced her was present for the morning service. During the prayers, several people — both men and women — stood up and offered the prayer 'Lord, help and save Miriam Pratt and all those who are being tortured in prison for conscience' sake'. Printed copies of her defence address were distributed outside the building. There were disturbances outside the Cathedral — over a decade later, Dorothy recalled how she had had her banner taken from her and her clothes nearly torn off her back.[16]

The demonstration in the Cathedral, together with Miriam's release, provoked a great deal of correspondence in the *Eastern Daily Press* in October and November 1913. An opponent wrote under the name 'Anti Humbug':

> *Dear me, are we to submit to our property being destroyed, our lives put in danger, our laws which are made for mutual protection set aside as of no moment, and then, when society insists on punishment for evil-doers, they whine and exclaim, you must not punish us because our consciences compelled us to do it.*

'WHJ' — undoubtedly Harry Jewson — replied by drawing wider social issues into the suffrage question:

> *The women's revolt is part of a widespread refusal to accept the conditions of modern life, a protest against unfair laws, against sweated work for men and women, against the mean and poor life which so many live, when a fuller and more human life is more possible for all.*

A writer calling himself Militant agreed:

> *The man who cannot see anything to admire in a young woman deliberately sacrificing her career and her liberty, and afterwards by the hunger strike risking her life, even though he could not approve of her act, that man in my opinion is much to be pitied.*

In February 1914 more WSPU meetings were held in Norwich. Nancy Lightman gave speeches at the Thatched Rooms and at the Bull Close Memorial Hall. On both occasions she had the support of an entertainment, a duologue called 'No 10 Clowning Street': no doubt this was Dorothy's contribution. Her brother Harry contributed yet again: he lent the Memorial Hall for the occasion, and also acted as chairman. More aggressive action continued alongside such peaceful activities: the pavilion on the Britannia Pier in Yarmouth was burnt down by suffragettes in April 1914.

The First World War changed everything. When it broke out on 4 August 1914, the WSPU suspended all political activity. A truce was declared: the prison sentences of women like Miriam Pratt were cancelled. Emmeline and Christabel Pankhurst were strong supporters of the war and of the duty — and right — of women to participate in it fully. Dorothy could not follow the Pankhursts' lead. As a pacifist she was totally against the war. Her new role was to help working women.

Britannia Pier Pavilion destroyed by suffragettes in 1914.

3

'The Destitute of Norwich and How they Live'

While Dorothy had been working for women's suffrage, she had also been working to help the lives of the very poorest in her city. In 1913, if you were unable to maintain yourself for whatever reason, whether through old age, illness or simple failure to find a job, your only recourse was to the Board of Guardians. They might force you into the city workhouse on Bowthorpe Road, or might pay you a pittance for you to live in your own house: often they would pay in goods such as flour rather than hand over money. There was a continual fear among the Guardians that men who could work might be shirking, preferring to take money from the ratepayers rather than work. For this reason adult males were never given out-relief: they would have either to go into the workhouse or work in the city's wood yard. Orphans and deserted children did not go into the workhouse but into separate Homes for Boys and Girls. Women left alone with children, whether widows, abandoned families or single mothers, also had nowhere to turn to apart from the Board of Guardians.

The Board of Guardians had 48 members, three from each district in the city. They were elected *en bloc* every three years. From the end of the nineteenth century, the occasional woman served on the Boards, including the Norwich Board: the first female Poor Law Guardians in the city were Emma Rump, Kate Mitchell and Alice Searle, all elected in December 1894.

Many people shared the view that the Board of Guardians was harsh in its treatment of the city's poor. Fred Jex of the Independent Labour Party recalled many years later how upset he was at the way that they treated people. He cited as an example 'a woman, her husband dying, she's got four children, and all the questioning, can't you get jobs even as charring in the morning when the children are at school? Bullying them into doing anything [rather] than looking after her'. Jex and others used to hold protest meetings at the Market Place on Sundays: these could attract as many as 500 people.[17]

The indignity that the poor were made to feel was at least as objectionable as the actual money involved. Edith Hill was still bitter in 1986, recalling an incident of seventy years earlier. Her father had died in 1912, leaving her mother with two young children:

> *If things got too bad one had to pluck up courage & go to the Board of Guardians. Once when my mother went to the Board of Guardians they allowed her two shillings for me. She told them to keep it and was promptly reported for her action.*[18]

Hawkins quotes a case of a widow who earned three shillings a week as a char. She had seven children, the eldest of whom was old enough to work, earning 3s 6d a week. After applying to the Guardians, she was allowed five shillings a week and flour for bread. The Society for the Prevention of Cruelty to Children charged her with neglecting the children; after investigation it was found that the money allowed by the Board was simply inadequate for the needs of the family.[19]

Dorothy's first involvement in Norwich politics sprang out of her concern for the city's poor, and her first election battle was for a seat on the Norwich Board of Guardians. In 1913 she published a booklet entitled *The Destitute of Norwich and How they Live*. This was compiled by a group of 'Investigators', who visited houses in the city and helped the occupants to fill in a questionnaire about household income and expenditure. Half a century later, one of the Investigators remembered their work:

> *A typical entry was a widow with five small children. She went out to work and earned 12 shillings. When she had paid her rent and someone to keep an eye on the children while she was at work, she had just over 8 shillings weekly to feed and clothe the five.*

Fifty-nine Investigators spent January and February 1912 looking at the conditions in which those on out-relief in the city were living. They considered 895 cases of people receiving out-relief, involving 2,050 people altogether. The great majority were families where the mother was a widow, or where the father was too ill to work: these made up 1,374 of the individuals concerned. The others were the sick, infirm and the elderly – single people of working age could not claim out-relief so they were not included in the Investigation.

Inevitably, the investigation took in some of the worst housing conditions in the city. Of the 895 families or individuals on out-relief, 54 lived in flats or houses where one water-closet was shared with four or more families, and 58 in accommodation where seven or more families shared a single water tap.

Many of the children were neglected, but not from the choice of the mother:

> We found that in 55 cases out of 306, where there were young children in the home, the mother was working regularly away from home. In some of these cases, the mother would be away from home the whole of the week during working hours, and in others several days of the week, cleaning or charring. In a few instances the children would be taken to a day nursery, and in others neighbours would look after them, but in a large number of cases it was evident that young children were allowed to play about in the streets the greater part of their time out of school, untended and uncared for.

The Investigators published sample household accounts, showing how these poor families spent their money, down to the last farthing. Rent and fuel (coal, oil, wood) took up most of the income. The spending on food was also detailed. By far the

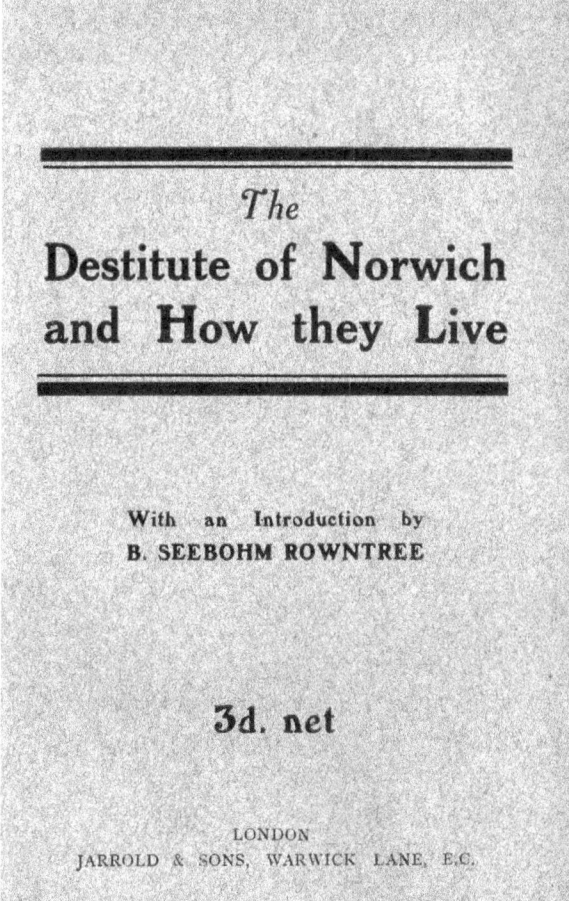

'The Destitute of Norwich and How They Live'

greatest expenditure was on bread, with either margarine or dripping and a small amount of jam and/or cheese. Tea, sugar, a little milk (more if there was a baby in the house), and infinitesimal quantities of meat, fish and vegetables took up the remainder of the money. Most of the women made small purchases of coal, bread and margarine every day at a local small general store: this was more expensive but the families could not afford to buy in larger quantities — and if the money ran out towards the end of the week, would simply have to go without. Many families could only afford to spend two or three pence a day on food for each child.

The diet a mother could provide for her children was simply inadequate:

> *A large number of children, while they have enough bread, with either cheap jam or margarine on it, doubtless cannot be given such a diet as that on which it is possible to rear physically sound and strong citizens. White bread, jam, and tea, and little else, is not a diet on which growing children can be brought up, though they may never actually suffer from hunger.*

Seerbohm Rowntree underlined this: such a diet, even with potatoes for supper, led to the slow exhaustion of the body from lack of nutriment:

> *the results of this insufficient diet must be looked for in the high death-rates in those quarters where the poor congregate, especially the deaths from consumption — which is so largely a disease of poverty — and the high infantile mortality.*

Mothers often did not even dare to put their children on the list for free school dinners in case the Guardians used it as an excuse to cut their benefits.

The booklet was published in the spring of 1912, and is an insight into how the poorest section of Norwich society lived. It carried a short Introduction by Rowntree, who wrote:

> *There is no graver spectacle in our modern town life than that of children, brought up in a slum, underfed throughout their childhood and adolescence, launched into unskilled careers for which they are physically unfitted, drifting first, perhaps, into regular and casual work, with intervals of loafing, and too often degenerating into cadgers, unemployables, or even criminals.*

Although the book is anonymous, one can feel the hands of Harry and Dorothy

'THE DESTITUTE OF NORWICH AND HOW THEY LIVE'

Jewson in it. The conclusion of the report is worth quoting in full:

> *It has been shown that the amount of out-relief given in Norwich at the present time is altogether insufficient to meet the necessities of a great many of the recipients. It is not economical to keep it at the low level, at which it now is, for we are simply rearing a generation, a large percentage of whom must turn out to be inefficient citizens as a result of the privations they are suffering. Moreover, it is not economical, because in many instances it is driving people into the House who might at a very much less cost be maintained on out-relief. We are afraid that in addition to the fact that relief is on an altogether too low basis, it is also the fact that there is inconsistency in dealing with many similar cases: accounts being settled with no clear principle, but by the whim of whatever happens to be the majority of the Relief Committee on any particular occasion. It is the individual elector and citizen who is responsible for this suffering and waste of human life. The future administration of out-relief in Norwich depends entirely upon what the will of the citizens is in this matter. The present Poor Law is admitted on all hands to be in many respects out of date, but we in Norwich can at*

A Norwich court: many of the poor lived in conditions like these.

> *any rate see to it that those children, widows, old and infirm people, who are being maintained on out-relief, shall live on a decent human footing by adopting such a minimum standard as we have suggested.*

The Investigators held a public meeting in March 1912 to launch the book, and passed a resolution:

> *As a result of our investigation into out-relief in Norwich . . . we are of opinion that in cases where there is no other income:*
> *Every adult should receive not less than five shillings per week.*
> *Every old couple, or two people agreeing to live together, should receive not less than ten shillings per week.*
> *Widows with dependent children, who are unable to go out to work, owing to their time being required to look after their children properly, should have five shillings per week. The amount for children should be four shillings for the first child, three shillings for the second child, and 2s 6d for each of the other children.*

The case had been proved, at least in the eyes of the Investigators; now was the time for action by the voters. The next election for places on the Board of Guardians was due in April 1913. The Investigators decided to put up candidates to oppose the current members of the Board. They put up eight candidates in different wards, standing mainly in Conservative and Liberal-held seats, as the few ILP people on the Board were in sympathy with their aims. The candidates included Dorothy and Harry, who both stood in Earlham ward, and Dorothy acted as spokesperson for the group.

The election was fought out in local meetings and in letters to the local press. The latter nearly all concerned Earlham ward: the Jewsons were clearly seen as the key players among the Investigators. Dorothy claimed that the usual 'dole' for a child of a widow was just two shillings a week, forcing the woman out to work. She added:

> *To keep people in the Workhouse, where they cost 8s 6d a week, who might have 5 shillings and live outside, is a policy as extravagant and cruel as it is to try to rear children who are chronically underfed and under-clothed. No common-sense person would tolerate it in the case of his or her own dependants. Why then do it in the case of those dependent on the City?*

One of the Board, Revd C. C. Lanchester, defended their position. He said the Board had very much increased the rates recently. Under Dorothy's proposal a widow with four children would receive 17 shillings a week. This was far too much:

> *There are many cases of men at work where the wage earner with himself to feed, and possibly more children, does not hand over this amount regularly for housekeeping. To give relief on a larger scale than the wages that are earned would, in fact, CREATE MORE EVIL THAN GOOD. It would tend to undermine the valuable spirit of self-dependence, discourage thrift, and increase the area of pauperism.*

Dorothy's proposals would also lead to a massive increase in the poor rate: this in itself 'would crush the hard-working and struggling ratepayer'.

Many letters in the press were written under pseudonyms. On 1 April, 'Worker' wrote that 'every voter in Earlham ward next Monday is either for a minimum standard of five shillings a week or against'. Harry wrote under his own name: 'it is revolting to think that widows and children for whom we as citizens are responsible are living in semi-starvation'. Mabel Clarkson, who was on the Board, described the pamphlet as 'exaggerated, unfair and inaccurate', but most people agreed with another letter writer who thought that the Investigators in putting together their pamphlet 'were investigating the heart and conscience of every elector in Norwich'.

The Investigators deliberately stood under that title and not for any political party, which also caused debate. 'Voter' called the Jewsons 'Socialists and faddists' but 'Liberal' responded: 'the minimum scale principles on which Miss and Mr Jewson stand are not in the least connected with Socialism . . . The fact is that the present scale of out-relief stands condemned in the eyes of Conservatives and Liberals alike'. He urged Liberals to support the 'enthusiastic candidature' of the Jewsons.

A writer calling himself 'X Travagant' indulged in irony: if a widow and four children got 17 shillings a week 'the poor woman would be so overburdened with her weekly income that she would be quite unable to dispose of it!' He had heard that there were 23 widows with four children in the city in 1912 and that the Board gave them on average 9s 4d a week, or almost two shillings per head: 'such lavish wealth to feed, clothe and house the citizens of tomorrow!'

At her final election meeting, held at Belvoir Street schoolroom, Dorothy criticised those people who said that it was pointless giving more money to the poor because they would only spend it on 'drink and dress: if that ever did happen, some of the relief could be given in food'.

BOARD OF GUARDIANS' ELECTION, LAKENHAM 1913

H. E. Hawes (Conservative)	547
Revd C. C. Lanchester (Conservative)	528
W. Whellum (Conservative)	514
W. H. Jewson (Independent)	478
Miss D. Jewson (Independent)	470

Unfortunately for Dorothy, the people entitled to vote in the election were those who would have to pay the poor rate rather than those who would receive the poor relief. Two of the Investigators *were* elected to the Board of Guardians, as were some Independent Labour Party candidates who supported the Investigators' demands, including Annie Reeves, Fred Jex and Walter Smith; however, Dorothy and her brother Harry were narrowly defeated by the three sitting Board members. The *Eastern Daily Press* praised the achievements of the Jewsons, pointing out that Earlham was one of the very best organised wards in the city. It carried two letters in its columns making the same point: one stressed that a few extra workers concentrating on the women voters in the ward might well have given them success.

In a tribute to Harry Jewson four years later, Revd A. Lowe, one of the successful candidates, said: 'the enterprise was not nearly resultless. It is bearing fruit today in a juster measure of out-relief for the poor of the city'. Half a century later, one of the Investigators still remembered their work with pride: 'there may be some things wrong with our society today, but at least our social conscience has somewhat improved, thanks to the example of such as Dorothy Jewson'.

A major step forward for women came on 1 November 1913, in the elections for the city council. The only woman candidate, Mabel Clarkson, defeated J. Youngs in Town Close ward by just 21 votes: for the first time ever there was a woman on the city council. In her election manifesto she wrote:

> I believe that the Best Wealth of a City is in the Health of its Citizens. I shall always be in favour of feeding Children who are in want; giving them a Good Education; paying the worker a Living Wage; caring for the Sick in the Hospitals; and Pensions for aged workers.

Dorothy would have agreed with these sentiments, but her time in politics was still to come.

4
Dorothy Jewson as pacifist and union worker
1914–1922

The outbreak of war in August 1914 took people by surprise. Most people in England supported the war, especially after Germany invaded Belgium – the defence of 'gallant little Belgium' was a very popular rallying call. The Labour Party was split by the war. Its leader, Ramsay MacDonald, and one of its constituent parts, the Independent Labour Party, declared themselves against the war. However, most of the members of the Labour Party were in favour of the war, including George Roberts, the Norwich Labour MP. MacDonald resigned as leader of the Party and was replaced by Arthur Henderson. Broadly speaking, the division was between the trade unionists, who were in favour of the war, and the members of the Independent Labour Party, who opposed it.

As a pacifist, Dorothy was of course instinctively opposed to the war; this must have caused some strain in her family and in her own heart. Her brother Harry had supported her suffrage campaign and stood with her as one of the Investigators. Now their paths were to diverge: Harry served with the 4th Norfolk Regiment.

As war loomed in August 1914, an anti-war demonstration was held on Sunday 2 August in Trafalgar Square in London. It was poorly attended compared with, say, the enormous demonstration against the war with Iraq in 2003, reflecting the general feeling in favour of war with Germany. Even its supporters only claimed a crowd of 20,000. There was an anti-war meeting in Norwich on the same Sunday, one of about 20 in British towns organised by the Independent Labour Party. It

The First World War toymakers — and the toys they made.

was held in the Market Place and its organisers included Witard, and also Fred Easton, who ran a bookshop in Pitt Street and was secretary of the Norwich Peace Association. Most people, however, including the great majority of the working class, saw all anti-war campaigners as cowards at best, German sympathisers at worst.

Dorothy began her war work in charge of a workshop for girls established by the Norwich Distress Committee to relieve unemployment. She volunteered to go to the Women's Emergency Corps in London and obtain information on how to set up a local toy factory. There was a direct link to this work from women's suffrage:

> *The Women's Emergency Corps — in whose ranks were to be found most of the women who had lately been making so brave a fight for Woman Suffrage — came to the conclusion that a field of industry lay open to the girls and women of our country in the making of wooden toys and stuffed dolls and animals, if the necessary instruction could be obtained; to this end, they established workrooms in which many women were trained as instructors in the art of 'toy-making'.*[20]

The Norwich workshop was in a room in St Margaret's parish lent by William Moore, the Chairman of the Board of Guardians. It was maintained by voluntary subscriptions. It began in November 1914 with 37 girls aged between fifteen and eighteen. Dorothy threw herself into her work (clearly any teaching/union work was taking a back seat): 'she is always at her post, from 8 o'clock in the morning till long after the girls have gone home in the evening — and her devotion to the work she has taken in hand and the energy she has put into it has inspired the girls with a real love for their work'. There was a Distress Committee in Norwich supplying work for both men and women in the early months of the war: their provision for women was in making clothes for soldiers. As a pacifist, Dorothy may well have found even this unpalatable: toy-making was a demonstrably peaceful occupation. Although the work was approved by the Distress Committee, it was not paid for by ratepayers but by voluntary subscriptions. At its peak, fifty-five unemployed girls and women found work with the toy makers: they worked a 44-hour week. They also rented a stall on the market on Saturdays as a retail outlet for the toys.

By chance, the ILP held its annual conference in Norwich in 1915. The two main speakers were Keir Hardie and Ramsay MacDonald. Because of its anti-war stance, most Norwich meeting-places refused to stage the Conference. The Party had booked the Thatched Assembly Rooms, with a Sunday meeting at the Hippodrome Theatre, but R. H. Bond, the owner of the former, cancelled the booking at short notice, and the Hippodrome followed suit. In the end, a Primitive Methodist minister, E. B. Storr, allowed them to use the schoolroom attached to his chapel in Queen's Road. They also had their own Hall in St Gregory's Alley, Norwich, known today as Keir Hardie Hall. It was family friendly, being described as early as 1910 as the only place in the city where a man could take his wife and children and have a beer in respectable circumstances. It was this building that ILP delegate Fenner Brockway recalled in his autobiography:

The Independent Labour Party Conference in Norwich, Easter 1915: welcoming committee.

> At night Norwich was pitch black; since it was a town near the East Coast not a light through the house windows or in the streets. As I approached the ILP Club I saw some ghostly white figures grouped together. Suddenly the strains of: 'O God, our Help in Ages Past' rose from them. The vicar had brought his choir to sing outside the hall in protest against the holding of an anti-war meeting.
>
> Hardie made this incident the theme of his opening speech. The little hall was crowded to suffocation and the lights were dimmed. Hardie's bushy white hair and his white beard shone out in the darkness with almost phosphorescent radiance. His head was held high, defiantly; his voice was strong and deep. His speech was the most uncompromising denunciation of war I had heard from him. Mass murder he called it, and the statesmen and parsons and Labour leaders who appealed for recruits were guilty of incitement to murder. His voice nearly broke when he spoke of the tragedy of Socialists murdering each other, but then he spoke confidently of the rebuilding of the International Socialist movement and of the final triumph of Socialism and the ending of war for all time.[21]

The ILP was always ready to listen to its women members, no doubt part of its appeal to Dorothy. One speaker from the platform was Katherine Glasier who spoke movingly of what the war was doing to the young:

> *Human solidarity is not a sloppy sentiment but a fact in nature . . . This is the darkest hour of the world's conscious life — the undoing of all the work of human parenting. We must dedicate ourselves to get children to become unselfish and to think of life as human service.'*

The Conference was followed almost immediately by an International Congress of Women, held at The Hague. The 156 British women on the Conference Committee included many known to Dorothy including Ethel Williams, a fellow pupil (some years earlier) at Dorothy's school and one of the earliest female doctors, and Mary Sheepshanks, daughter of the Bishop of Norwich and one of the first trained social workers. Dorothy was in full sympathy with their objectives:

1   To demand that International disputes shall in future be settled by some other means than war.

2   To claim that women should have a voice in the affairs of the nations.

Significantly, the women who were to form the centre of the next part of Dorothy's life were involved: Margaret Bondfield and Marion Phillips were among the four British women to attend the Conference, Mary Macarthur and Susan Lawrence were on the Committee.

The first flush of enthusiasm among the toymakers died away as it became clear that there would be plenty of essential work for women in the wartime economy. By the end of 1915 there were only fifteen girls working on toys at the Norwich workshop. It was time for Dorothy to move on. In 1916 she moved to London, setting up home at Mecklenburgh Square in Bloomsbury — 'beautiful Mecklenburgh Square' she was to call it, forty years later. Her new job was to help organise the National Federation of Women Workers. This had been founded ten years earlier by Mary Macarthur to encourage women to join the union movement: it was an offshoot of the Women's Trade Union League, of which Marion Phillips was organiser. The Federation had struggled at first — 'jobs were scarce and women six a penny', Dorothy later recalled.

One of Fed's earliest workers was Maud Murray, who was to become Dorothy's friend and companion for twenty years. People like Dorothy Jewson were 'champagne socialists' — wealthy women drawn into the cause. Maud Murray was different. Just a year younger than Dorothy, she was born in Islington in 1883, one of three daughters of George and Annie Murray. He was a sugar boiler, and clearly enjoyed alliteration: the full name he gave to his child was Maud Millicent Macpherson Murray. By the time Maud was seventeen she was living in Barnsbury, Islington, with her aunt, Emily Wren, and both were working in a cartridge factory. Ten years later, they had moved together to Tottenham, still working in munitions — Emily was a forewoman ammunition worker, Maud a cartridge case maker. Maud had thus been working

Publicity photo, engineering jobs for women.

for many years in an industry that after 1914 suddenly became a major employer of women — her experience of employment practices and working conditions must have been invaluable to the union leaders.

Dorothy recalled that when Maud joined there was still only one branch of the union. Maud was one of the first women to 'become so enthusiastic that they volunteered to join M. M. in going to other factories to persuade women there to join'. At some factories these enthusiasts were pelted by women workers who did not want a union, but the foundations were laid and more branches were founded: 'as Fed grew Mary Macarthur gathered round her men and women'.

Another recruit was Susan Lawrence, a former Conservative who became active in Labour politics in London after her conversion to the cause in 1912. Like Dorothy, she was definitely not working class: in fact she was distinctly aristocratic — Mary Macarthur used to tell Dorothy stories of how Susan 'drove up in her carriage and pair, coachman and footman, all in state'. Not surprisingly, the Federation was at first regarded as a middle class organ for charity: however, it grew from just 2,000 members in 1906 to 20,000 in 1914.

The war years saw the rapid development of the Federation. It came into its own during the War, when many thousands of women took places left by men in engineering, especially in munitions. Conditions were unpleasant — munitions workers were nicknamed 'canaries' as the work turned their skin yellow. It was also very dangerous — a large number of girls and women were killed in explosions in munitions factories, largely forgotten heroes of the war. As Dorothy recalled 'women were put onto munitions at low pay, long hours and appalling conditions'. Many branches were formed. Sympathetic MPs, including Mary's husband Will Anderson, managed to ensure that a minimum wage rate was established by law, and this was later raised as wartime inflation began to bite. The Federation took employers who were not paying the minimum wage before Special Arbitration Tribunals, who enforced the rate, with back-pay where appropriate.[22]

Dorothy played an important role within the union, especially as Mary Macarthur was combining her trade union work with being a mother: her daughter Anne Elizabeth ('Nancy') had been born in 1915. Dorothy recalled fifty years later that, however, busy Mary was, she would stop at five each evening for her daughter's bath! Looking back on her union work, she wrote: 'Women before had been scared of [the] sack. Now they gained confidence and learned. We had to teach them to write and to educate them to play their part in TU [trade union] and Labour movement'.

The type of work in which she was involved during the war can be typified by the

Banner of the National Federation of Women Workers.

case of Florence Hammond. Florence worked in munitions and at Christmas in 1917 she and other girls went on strike over wages. When they did not return to work after the Christmas break, the girls were dismissed. They claimed the right to the payment of a week's wages and with the support of 'Fed' took the case to the District Tribunal, where their claim was upheld. The case dragged on after the war: the company's appeal against the decision of the tribunal was finally heard in 1919. During the 1919 hearing, Dorothy appeared in the Law Courts as the first lady advocate. The judge said that under the rules she was not entitled to appear in this role but only as a friend — however she made use of the opportunity to advise her client and she was successful: the judge dismissed the final appeal by the employers.[23]

It was not just munitions workers who were supported by the union: in 1919, waitresses in tea shops, restaurants and hotels protested at their conditions of work: they wanted a minimum wage of 35 shillings and a maximum working week of 44 hours. In her role as Organising Secretary for the Union, Dorothy spoke on their behalf when they threatened to strike.[24]

Dorothy noted that women workers had been terrified of the sack before the war: now they were gaining confidence, learning to read and write, and were becoming educated to play their part in the union movement.

Women also had to struggle to gain recognition within the Labour Party. Dorothy recalled:

> I remember an early Lab conference when we had 10 women delegates from Fed. We were put away up in the Gallery. The body of the hall was filled mostly with men . . . One of our delegates, a little woman from Barrow, a fighter, got up and asked a question on some small point. The Chairman ignored her. Mary stood up, a towering angry figure, shouting to the Chairman — 'had he not realised one of her delegates wished to speak?' All eyes turned up to look. Electricity was in the air. Chairman apologised. Two points registered. Fed was there and women were in future not to be ignored.

In her union work, Dorothy worked with Mary Macarthur and Susan Lawrence, as we have seen, and also with Margaret Bondfield. All four women were totally opposed to the war. Emmeline Pankhurst, in contrast, was strongly in favour of the war, and therefore moved into direct opposition to Dorothy and her new associates: Macarthur and Bondfield were described by Emmeline as 'Bolshevik women trade union leaders'.

During the war, Dorothy suffered a great personal loss. Harry had served at Gallipoli, and later in Egypt, where he spent his spare half-hours trying to learn Arabic. The regiment then fought in Palestine; Harry was killed at Gaza on 19

April 1917. He was hit three times during an attack and badly wounded: he lay out in the open for two hours in the hot sun. Eventually he tried to make it back but was hit once more: according to his servant, who was with him, his last words were 'Give my love to my people'. A memorial service for him and a friend, Captain Page, killed in the same attack, was held at Princes Street Congregational Chapel in Norwich on 6 May. Dorothy was present: then it was back to London to continue her very different kind of war work.

Harry Jewson, Dorothy's eldest brother and fellow 'Investigator'.

Women had done great work in munitions and other factory work during the war, but, once the war was over, the returning soldiers wanted their jobs back. It was a difficult time for women workers: there were over 650,000 unemployed women by early 1919. Many could not even obtain unemployment benefit: those, including highly-skilled workers, who refused to take positions in domestic service were refused benefit. Dorothy was one of the leaders of a 'Fed' deputation to the Minister of Labour

George Roberts MP striking a military pose in Norwich Market Place.

THE NATIONAL FEDERATION OF WOMEN WORKERS

WOMEN WORKERS' (1919) CHARTER

PROCLAMATION
at the Royal Albert Hall Saturday, Feb. 15th, 1919 at 7.30 p.m.

PROGRAMME—PRICE ONE PENNY

The Executive Committee desire to thank:

Those FREE HOLDERS who have placed their boxes and stalls at the disposal of the Federation.

The HERALD for generous support and co-operation.

Miss Dorothy Jewson (Organiser of the Meeting), Mrs. Ayrton Gould, the Organisers, the Stewards, and all who have contributed to make the gathering worthy of its high object.

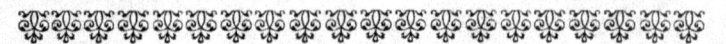

The 1919 Albert Hall meeting.

protesting about this. They also demanded that munitions factories — and their workers — be used to build houses and housing accessories, but nothing was done.

Dorothy organised a great meeting at the Royal Albert Hall on 15 February 1919 to proclaim a Women Workers' Charter. This was to be a fully Socialist event: 'The Red Flag' was sung, and the meeting ended with 'God Save Our People' rather than 'God Save the King'. Mary Macarthur and Susan Lawrence were among the speakers. The charter made demands still relevant today, almost a century later. It had three elements:

1 THE RIGHT TO WORK: *the provision of suitable work or full maintenance for all workers, whether by hand or brain.*

2 THE RIGHT TO LIFE: *security against want: and a wage sufficient to maintain health and happiness.*

3 THE RIGHT TO LEISURE: *time to think, and play, and do things.*

The charter demanded equal consideration for clerical and professional workers, and pledged to work 'against any sex or class distinctions'. It demanded a legal basic wage 'sufficient to provide all the requirements of a full development of body, mind and character'. It called for a maximum working day of eight hours and a maximum working week of 40 hours 'so that full opportunity for recreation and physical and mental development may be available for all'. It was also Dorothy who represented 'Fed' at a Government Committee of Enquiry in December 1919.

Mary Macarthur suffered a severe blow when her husband died of influenza in 1919. She herself died of cancer in 1921 at the age of 40. To Dorothy it was a great loss. Forty years later she wrote of Mary: 'she was a figure of great dignity and charm and she had moreover an inward spiritual grace that illumined her actions and made her a great personality'. By the time of her death, the Federation had grown to 146 branches and 54,000 members 'but its beloved leader fell ill and was taken at a time when TU and Lab movement needed most her clear insight and instrumental knowledge of it'. Margaret Bondfield stepped into her shoes as President of the Federation, but later in the year it ceased to exist as an independent all-woman organisation, amalgamating with the National Union of General and Municipal Workers. This meant a new role for Dorothy: she now worked as organiser for the women's section of this Union.

The year 1921 was also a dramatic one for George Lansbury and Susan Lawrence: they were both put in prison for their part in trying to improve the lot of the poor in Poplar. They were among thirty Labour councillors and Guardians of the Poor 'imprisoned for dealing with the unemployed through generous relief scales and for ignoring the rules and regulations governing the provision of relief'. Lansbury spent four months in Pentonville, Susan five weeks in Holloway: her offence was to refuse to collect the Poor Rate. Dorothy sardonically suggested that prison life improved her: 'she had to get up early and clean her cell — keep regular hours — rest and above all no cigs. She looked better on her return'.

At the end of the war the suffragette cause was assured of victory: in 1918 the right to vote was given to all men over 21 and to women over 30, provided that they were householders or wives of householders: these restrictions were put in so that women voters would not be in the majority. Some women leaders, such as Sylvia Pankhurst and Mary Macarthur, were unwilling to accept this limited suffrage for women. However, as the majority of the supporters of women's suffrage recognised, it was bound to be only temporary. Mary Macarthur actually stood for Parliament in the General Election of 1918, for the Labour Party of course, one of their four women candidates: she lost by 1,333 votes, a defeat she attributed to the fact that the returning officer would not let her call herself Mary Macarthur on the ballot paper, insisting she be put down as Mrs Anderson.

Women were also making progress in local government. More women gained seats on Norwich City Council after the war: there were five by 1921. In 1920, when Mrs Henderson joined her husband on Norwich City Council, they became the first married couple in Britain to serve together on the same municipal council. In November 1923, Ethel Colman was appointed Lord Mayor of Norwich, the first female Lord Mayor in England; her sister Helen acted as Lady Mayoress. They were daughters of James Jeremiah Colman, the mustard manufacturer and former Liberal MP. The *Eastern Daily Press* said 'Miss Ethel Colman is the first lady Lord Mayor of Norwich, but we are quite sure that long before the end of her year of office, the citizens will determine that she shall not be the last'.[25]

By 1922, after only four years of recruitment, one hundred thousand women had joined local branches of the Labour Party: these were the troops to fight the 1923 general election. The party had achieved this while distancing itself from women-only organisations in favour of a united struggle by both sexes: in 1925 the party only narrowly rejected a proposal to ban women from being members of the Labour Party if they were in women-only organisations like the National Union of Societies for Equal Citizenship. Dorothy was a member of this group, the successor to Millicent Fawcett's NUWSS, being created in 1919 with Millicent as President. It has been called 'the major feminist pressure group in the 1920s: its programme included both equalisation of the franchise and equal pay for equal work'.[26]

Throughout her career, Dorothy was a strong supporter of women-only groups: she played a key role at many Women's Labour Party conferences, which were held every year from 1918. Labour Party historian Martin Pugh describes her as one of the 'middle-class labour feminists' who 'believed that women should retain independent organisations for fear of being absorbed and exploited by male-dominated parties.

They reflected the attitudes and experience of the Edwardian generation of suffragists'.[27]

Dorothy's father did not live to see Ethel Colman's appointment as mayor or Dorothy's campaign to become the city's first female Member of Parliament: George Jewson died on 23 March 1923 at the age of 75. There was a private funeral service at Tower House, Mary being too ill to go to the public funeral which followed at the Rosary Cemetery, where he was buried in a family plot with members of his wife's family, the Jarrolds. His will, rewritten after Harry's death, named his sole surviving son Christopher as executor, along with George's brother, Frank Jewson. The family money was put into trusts to support Mary: after her death £8,000 was to go to each daughter, the rest to Christopher. Any daughter still unmarried at the time of his wife's death was to receive the family furniture and plate: at the time of George's death none of his three surviving daughters, including Dorothy, were married. George had been head of Jewson's for over forty years, and had become Chairman when it had been formed into a Limited Liability Company. His brother William succeeded him as Chairman, but just four months later he too died. He was succeeded by a third brother, Frank Jewson.

Ethel Colman, the country's first female lord mayor.

5

The 1923 General Election in Norwich

In 1923, Prime Minister Stanley Baldwin decided to call a general Election on a specific issue: Protection (putting tariffs on imported goods to encourage people to 'buy British'). At the 1922 election, the previous Prime Minister, Arthur Bonar Law, had specifically promised an election if protectionist policies were introduced, and his successor felt bound to honour this.

Norwich was a double-member constituency: all electors had two votes and the two names topping the poll were elected. Naturally people tended to vote for two candidates from the same party if they could (on many occasions the parties did not all field two candidates), but there were always some voters who did not. They might cast just one vote (plumping) or they might vote for one candidate from one party and a second from another (cross-voting): in a close election votes from these groups could mean the difference between success and failure.

In Norwich in 1923, all three major parties were able to put up two candidates. The Conservatives had George Roberts, who had won three elections in Norwich as a Labour candidate, one as a National Liberal and one as an Independent: he had now moved decisively to the right. Alongside him they fielded H. D. Swan, chiefly known as a former county cricketer for Essex. The Liberals also already had one sitting member – Edward Hilton Young. On 19 November they announced their second candidate, Henry Copeman, the head of the provision merchant firm and leader of the Liberal party on the City Council.

Labour turned to Walter Smith and Dorothy Jewson. Smith had been prominent

PARLIAMENTARY ELECTION, 1923.

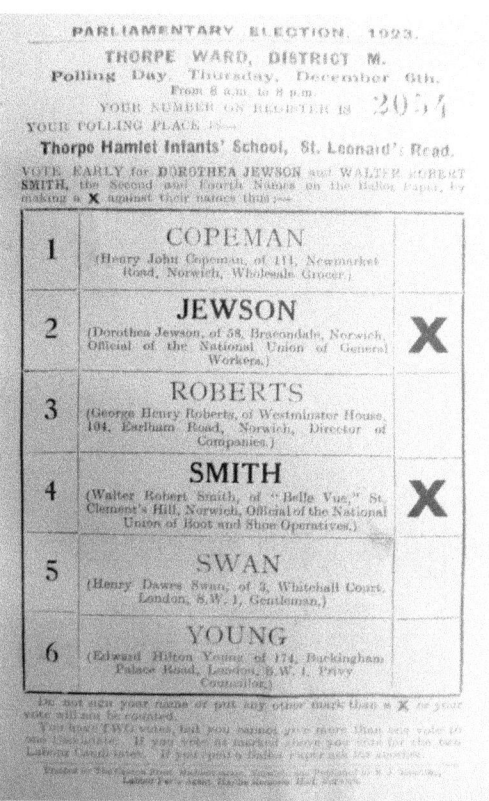

THORPE WARD, DISTRICT M.
Polling Day, Thursday, December 6th.
From 8 a.m. to 8 p.m.
YOUR NUMBER ON REGISTER IS 2054
YOUR POLLING PLACE IS—
Thorpe Hamlet Infants' School, St. Leonard's Road.

VOTE EARLY for DOROTHEA JEWSON and WALTER ROBERT SMITH, the Second and Fourth Names on the Ballot Paper, by making a X against their names thus:—

1	COPEMAN (Henry John Copeman, of 111, Newmarket Road, Norwich, Wholesale Grocer.)	
2	JEWSON (Dorothea Jewson, of 58, Bracondale, Norwich, Official of the National Union of General Workers.)	X
3	ROBERTS (George Henry Roberts, of Westminster House, 104, Earlham Road, Norwich, Director of Companies.)	
4	SMITH (Walter Robert Smith, of "Belle Vue," St. Clement's Hill, Norwich, Official of the National Union of Boot and Shoe Operatives.)	X
5	SWAN (Henry Dawes Swan, of 3, Whitehall Court, London, S.W. 1, Gentleman.)	
6	YOUNG (Edward Hilton Young, of 174, Buckingham Palace Road, London, S.W. 1, Privy Councillor.)	

in Norwich local government. He was a union man, being both President of the National Union of Agricultural Workers and an official of the National Union of Boot and Shoe Trade operatives. He also had Parliamentary experience, having been Labour MP for Wellingborough between 1918 and 1922.

The historian Martin Pugh thinks that in double constituencies like Norwich it was a deliberate tactic by the Labour Party 'to extend its appeal among voters by combining a standard male trade unionist with a middle class woman'. However, Dorothy cannot be simply described as middle class. As we have seen, she was also from the trade union world. The local press

How Norfolk & Suffolk Voted.

CONSERVATIVE VICTORY IN S.W.

The "Red Flag" at Aylsham.

NORWICH.

Norwich election result was announced late on Friday afternoon as follows:—

W. R. SMITH (Lab.) 20,077
DOROTHY JEWSON (Lab.) 19,304
E. HILTON YOUNG (L)... 16,222
G. H. ROBERTS (C) 14,749
H. J. COPEMAN (L) 13,180
H. D. SWAN (C)... 12,713

Labour gains two seats, one Liberal and one Conservative, for though Mr. Roberts was elected in November, 1922, as an Independent, he had since gone over to the Conservative Party. The Right Hon. G. H. Roberts has been a member for Norwich since 1906, and has been in office as a Lord Commissioner of the Treasury, Parliamentary Secretary to the Board of Trade, Minister of Labour, and Food Controller. The Right Hon. E. Hilton Young, D.S.O., has been member for Norwich since 1915 and has served the office of Financial Secretary to the Treasury.

The following analysis of the voting is interesting:—

Copeman and Young 12,765
Jewson and Smith 18,588
Roberts and Swan 12,112
Copeman 75
Jewson 179
Roberts 321
Smith 294
Swan 104
Young 352
Copeman and Jewson 146
Copeman and Roberts 64
Copeman and Smith 102
Copeman and Swan 28
Jewson and Roberts 100
Jewson and Swan 83
Jewson and Young 208
Roberts and Smith... 285
Roberts and Young 1,867
Smith and Swan 82
Smith and Young 726
Swan and Young 304

Total 48,785

The number of votes cast, 48,785, makes 79.7 per cent. of the electorate (61,168) as compared with 78.5 per cent. polled at the election of November, 1922.

SOUTH.

G. EDWARDS (Lab.) 11,682
†MAJOR T. W. HAY (C.) ... 10,821

Majority 861
Labour gain.

Last year's figures:—
Hay (C.) 12,734
Edwards (Lab.) 10,159

The result was declared by Mr. A. Wansborough Jones, the Returning-officer, at 2.35.

AT WYMONDHAM.

Mr. George Edwards, M.P., was given a tremendous reception by his supporters on his arrival at Wymondham Labour Institute. Ropes were attached to the car, and headed by the New Buckenham Brass Band a procession was formed, the principal streets in the town being paraded. On arriving at the Fairlane Hall, Mr. Edwards found a crowded audience to receive him with much cheering.

Mr. George Edwards said that after three week's strenuous work he did not intend to say much, only to thank those who had worked so hard to secure such a splendid victory, also to thank his noble friend, Lord Kimberley, for the work and sacrifice he had made on his behalf.

EAST.

THE "CAPTAIN" BOWLED.

The result of the election in East Norfolk was announced at the Shirehall, Norwich, shortly after four o'clock, by Mr. C. Row, the Deputy Returning Officer.

SEELY (L.) 11,807
FALCON (C.) 8,472
HEWITT (Lab.) 3,530

Liberal gain.

1922 figures:—
Falcon (C.) 9,270
Seely (L.) 8,962
Hewitt (Lab.) 4,561

After the count Mr. H. M. Seely proposed a vote of thanks to the Returning Officer.

Mr. M. Falcon, in seconding, congratulated his opponent, remarking that at any rate East Norfolk would be represented by a member, part of whose name was Michael. (Laughter).

also stressed her feminist background — 'she was prominent some years ago as a militant suffragette'. She herself had some experience of the conditions of working women, as she explained at one campaign meeting. She had worked as a housemaid in a big London hotel: the women started work at 6 am and did not finish until nine at night. They were allowed two hours' break between five and seven, but were so exhausted they just went to their bedrooms to rest. For this she was paid fifteen shillings a week, with 3s 6d beer money. 'My room, high up on the tenth floor, had five beds'. The food was execrable: 'For breakfast we got stale bread left over from the visitors' tables, margarine of the very poorest quality and either sausages, cold porridge or kippers. It was always the same unvarying diet'.

Dorothy Jewson campaigning in 1923: the baby is Herbert Witard, nephew of the politician of that name.

Dorothy in the 1923 campaign; beside her is Walter Smith.

Dinner was so unappetising that the girls used up their hard-earned wages on buying their own. As Dorothy came from one of the wealthiest families in Norwich, some of her listeners were sceptical as to her experience of working life.[28]

The election campaign was short and sharp. On 16 November, Dorothy arrived at Trowse station from London. Throughout her campaign, she had the support of Maud Murray, who went to all the election meetings with her.[29]

Dorothy laid stress on women's issues, saying: 'I have been working amongst women – working women – particularly in my trade union activities since 1911' and went on to declare 'I think that the women's point of view needs to be put in Parliament. Unemployment among women is very much on the increase. There are 41,000 more women unemployed now than there were when the present Government came to power last December, and absolutely nothing has been done by the Government for them . . . There are 27,000 women electors [in Norwich] and 33,000 men electors, so it is not much to expect that there should be one woman when there are four or five men candidates'.

Two days later Margaret Bondfield, now President of the women's branch of the TUC, addressed a large crowd at the Electric Theatre. She said that the election would be fought not on the tariff question but on unemployment. Labour proposed a capital levy on personal fortunes of over £5,000 – she did not think that many of those present would have to pay it!

The Labour candidates were formally announced at a mass meeting at St Andrew's Hall on 20 November. Dorothy said:

> *it was not many years ago when the sight of a woman on the public platform meant cries from all citizens 'Go home to your children' or 'Cook your husband's dinner', quite regardless of the fact that the woman might not have either husband or children. (Laughter). Perhaps as one who had worked for the empowerment of her sex she ought to congratulate her city on showering honours on some of her sex after a very long time. They had a woman Lord Mayor (Applause). Mrs Colman had led the way, and it was to be hoped that the city might yet have a woman MP . . . A greater honour had been done her by asking her to stand, not as a woman, but as a representative of the organised workers of the city (Applause). It was of that she was most proud.*

On 22 November, there was a Labour meeting at the Quayside School. Dorothy said that at the last election an old man had told her that he would never vote for a petticoat. To general laughter, she said that people who talked like that did not realise what a terrible lot of old women there were in the House of Commons. She said that

Labour wanted every woman to have maintenance after childbirth – the Government had promised this, but had never carried it out. She defended the capital levy: 'A man with a fortune of £6000 would have to pay £50. Was that too much to ask of the men who were urging young men to go into the firing line? It was because it touched their pockets and because they knew the rich would have to pay, that Labour's opponents were fighting it with all their force'. On the next day, she spoke at the Avenue Road School. The chairman reminded her audience that she and her brother had done splendid work in exposing flaws in the administration of the Poor Law system in Norwich. Dorothy said that she had been visiting the poorer parts of the Wensum ward and was astonished by the housing conditions – far worse than before the war.

On another occasion, Dorothy spoke to a meeting of the city's unemployed, speaking of her 'deep sense of shame – shame that there should be in such a wealthy country as England so great an injustice as this enormous army of men and women who had not the means of working'. She talked about her own life in a way that clearly moved the crowd:

> *There was no reason why I should not come home to Norwich and enjoy every comfort, because I belong to the employing class, because I was one of the privileged . . . I say that every man should have the same choice – every boy and girl should have the same chance that I had . . . I was quite an ordinary girl, but I was allowed to go on to the university. It was at the university that I joined a Socialist society. And ever since then I have tried to work to secure the removal of the inequalities that exist in our society – the removal of the terrible feeling of insecurity that threatens many of you if you are unemployed.*

On 29 November, all six candidates were given the opportunity to make a 15-minute speech before the Norfolk and Norwich Branch of the National Council of Women. Dorothy said that she had given a good deal of her life to fighting for equal opportunities for women. More women were needed in the House of Commons to deal with such matters.

The Times of 30 November carried a report on Norwich suggesting that there might be a split result: 'as the candidates are in pairs the race is more like a chariot race than a horse race . . . [however] it may happen that one of the riders from two of the competing chariots may win – each, as it were, jumping from his car and by his personal merits reaching the winning-post on foot'. The same newspaper also cleared up the mystery of Dorothy's claim to have worked in service; she had worked briefly at a London hotel to discover for herself what the conditions were like: 'I was only there three weeks', she said; 'it was not long but it was long enough'.

The result was a triumph for the Labour Party:

1923 GENERAL ELECTION

Smith (Labour)	20,077
Jewson (Labour)	19,304
Young (Liberal)	16,222
Roberts (Consservative)	14,479
Copeman (Liberal)	13,180
Swan (Conservative)	12,713

Dorothy was interviewed for the local paper, the reporter asking whether, after a strenuous campaign, she would now take a rest: she smiled and replied, 'Oh, dear, no! I am anxious to get to work'. She commented, 'I know that the women in the poorer parts of Norwich turned out in their thousands to vote for me. From the yards of Coslany, Wensum, and the other poorer wards they went to the poll for me in a manner that was absolutely marvellous'.

Thirty-four of the 1,380 candidates at the 1923 election were women; eight were elected. Three of them were Labour MPs – Dorothy and her friends and fellow unionists Margaret Bondfield and Susan Lawrence. These three disciples of Mary Macarthur were the first female Labour MPs. Dorothy could claim that she had the highest vote of any of them – double member constituencies naturally had a larger electorate than other constituencies. Along with the Liberal Lady Terrington, also elected in 1923, they were also the first women MPs to be elected without 'inheriting' their seat from a husband. At 39, Dorothy was the youngest; Margaret Bondfield was 50 and Susan Lawrence 53 at the time of the election.

Dorothy and six of the other women met together in January 1924. Susan Lawrence was unable to attend but said that they had decided against a formal agreement to act as a women's party, but hoped they would be able to work together on women's issues: there would be no need to divide the rooms in Westminster allocated to women into 'Government' and 'Opposition'. In the new Government, Margaret Bondfield was the first ever woman appointed to a ministerial post. Lady Astor commented that she should have been put into the Cabinet but it was a start: women were on their way.

6

Dorothy in Parliament
1923–24

After the election, the Conservatives were the largest party, but would be defeated if the other parties voted against them. Baldwin tried to form a government but he was indeed defeated. The king's position was clear: he called for the leader of the next largest party, James Ramsay MacDonald, and asked him to form a government. On 22 January 1924 he did so: Labour was in government for the first time. King George wrote in his diary: 'Today 23 years ago dear Grandmamma [Queen Victoria] died. I wonder what she would have thought of a Labour government'.

However, although Labour was in government it did not have an overall majority, so its power was limited. Conservatives and Liberals could combine at any time to defeat the government. MacDonald and his cabinet favoured a cautious approach: they wanted to convince voters that Labour was a responsible party that could be trusted to govern the country.

Even before the Labour government was formed, Dorothy achieved publicity by taking part in an epic journey. She and Maud were in London in January 1924, where Dorothy took her oath of office. They needed to get back to Norwich but there was a rail strike on: some trains were running but to Dorothy those manning them were blacklegs trying to break a legitimate strike. Wishing to support the strikers, they decided to walk! They left on Sunday and, by means of various buses got as far as Brentwood, where they spent the night. They set off again on Monday morning and by a combination of walking and hitch-hiking they reached Halstead that night and Bury St Edmunds the following night: they stayed at the well-known Angel Hotel. They had travelled on foot and had had lifts in lorries, farmers' carts, brewers' drays and furniture vans. While at Bury they found out that the rail strike was over, and next day they finished their journey to Norwich by train. Not all that great a feat – they actually walked about 20 miles on the Monday and a little less on the Tuesday – but a good opportunity to show solidarity with the workers and to stress the virtues of the simple life: all they took with them on their journey was some bread, a piece of cheese, butter, figs and oranges. The press was approving: 'Both Miss Jewson and her companion looked very fit when they arrived, and said they had enjoyed the walk immensely'.

The Parliament was enlivened by a group of left wing Members of Parliament who were members of the ILP and who wanted a very radical programme of reform to be introduced by the Government. They were mainly from Glasgow and included James Maxton, John Wheatley and Campbell Stephen, a minister of the United Free Church who was to figure in Dorothy's later life. Stephen was born in Bower, Caithness in 1884. He is described by one writer as: 'stout, clean-shaven, with a good head of curly hair and a large smooth face with regular features'. MacDonald did not take to him, once referring to him as 'that damned little swine'. In April 1923, Maxton described a Conservative MP who supported a Government motion to cut health grants as a 'murderer'. There was uproar in the House and Maxton, Wheatley and Stephen were suspended. Dorothy was very much in sympathy with this group.[30]

During her time in Parliament, Dorothy was a very active MP, and was on the Liaison Committee between the Parliamentary Labour Party and the Cabinet. She also served on the House of Commons Kitchen Committee. In Parliament, she spoke mainly on women's and family matters. Her maiden speech was on 29 February, in support of a motion to reduce the voting age for women from 30 to 21. Taking note of the date, the proposer, W. M. Adamson, said the idea had been called a Leap Year proposal – 'I rather think however that if it had been a Leap Year Proposal, probably one of the lady members of the House would have been in the fortunate position of putting it forward'. Dorothy was next to speak. She condemned the law as it stood, and, naturally, she was especially interested in the position of mothers and working women:

> *I wish to draw attention to the very great injustice that is done to large bodies of women by their exclusion from the franchise. There is a large body of young wives and mothers who feel, very naturally, that if they are capable of bringing children into the world, and of being responsible to the State for those children, it is only right that they should have the privilege and protection of the vote in helping to mould the laws which will govern themselves and their children. Then there is the large body of wage-earning women. It is estimated that 70 per cent of those women are under 30 years of age and are now excluded from the franchise. They have suffered intensely, and are now suffering, from low wages and under-employment, and as this House will be discussing during the next few years questions of a minimum*

wage, hours of work and other questions which vitally affect these women, the time has come when they should have some opportunity of exercising their control over the laws that are going to affect them. There are also large numbers of wage-earning women, professional women, business women, nurses, governesses and a large body of hotel and domestic workers who are altogether excluded, or practically excluded, from the exercise of the vote. It may be argued that domestic workers have not any knowledge of politics, and should, therefore, be excluded, but I do not think that is a fair argument, because the women have shown in exercising the vote that they have gained knowledge and that the vote in itself has been a liberal education for them.

Dorothy's maiden speech was a great success: three other speakers — the Liberal MPs Margaret Wintringham, Isaac Foot and the Conservative Sir Robert Chadwick — all went out of their way to congratulate her. The motion was carried, and the bill committed to a Standing Committee. However, it did not become law until 1928. In March she looked at another aspect of women's suffrage: she was one of the sponsors of a bill to allow peeresses to sit and vote in the House of Lords.

In April, Dorothy spoke on another subject dear to her heart, children's welfare. This was in support of a bill giving both parents equal rights of guardianship. The second reading was moved by Mrs Wintringham. She pointed to a paradox in the law as it stood — wives had no right to say where their children were to live or to be educated. However, the mothers of illegitimate children did have these rights! Dorothy supported her and pointed out that another right that wives were denied was that of having a say in the religion in which their children were brought up: 'It is utterly unfair and illogical for the woman, who has the pain and responsibility of bringing the children into the world and looking after them in their early days, particularly the working woman, who has everything to do for the child and is nurse and governess, domestic servant and everything, that she should not have equal rights as well as equal responsibilities'. Dorothy used the occasion to make explicit her views on equality: 'Modern opinion recognises husband and wife to be equal parties . . . A woman is an equal citizen with a man'. The bill was read a second time and committed to a Standing Committee.

Dorothy's interest in family and children was recognised: she was one of five members of a Committee set up by the Home Secretary to look into the adoption of children in April, and in the same month was one of a group of MPs and others invited to lay foundation stones at a new maternity home being built by the Ilford Urban Council in Hatch Lane Ilford at a cost of £25,000.[31]

Radical MPs in this Parliament also tackled another issue, that of capital punishment. Dorothy had always opposed this, and she was part of a deputation to the Home Secretary in March. She also backed an unsuccessful bill for its abolition. The campaign was forty years before its time: indeed, Dorothy did not live to see its abolition in the 1960s.

The single issue with which Dorothy became most closely associated with during her time as an MP – and later – was the dissemination of information about birth control to working class women. In 1922, maternity clinics had been banned from giving out such information. The 1923 Labour Women's Conference voted in favour of providing full birth control information to everyone. One leading campaigner was Stella Browne, whom Dorothy had met when she had a temporary job with Fed in 1918. In April 1924, Dorothy invited Stella to Norwich where she held five women-only meetings and one for members of the ILP: Stella stayed with Dorothy's cousin, Violet Jewson, a doctor by profession.

On 9 May, Dorothy was part of a delegation to John Wheatley, the Health Minister: other delegates included the writer H. G. Wells and Dora Russell, wife of the philosopher Bertrand Russell. They demanded that Ministry of Health institutions should give contraceptive advice to those who asked for it, and that doctors at medical centres should be allowed to offer advice in certain medical cases. Dora Russell provocatively said that it was four times as dangerous for a woman to have a baby as it was for a man to work in a coal mine. (Wells asked Dora if she was sure of this and Dora produced the figures: on average, four or five mothers died in childbirth in every thousand births; 'only' 1.1 miners out of every thousand engaged actively in mining were killed in pit accidents.) On this issue, Dorothy found herself in opposition to Marion Phillips, now Chief Woman Officer to the Labour Party, who thought the dispute could split the Party.

The 1924 Women's Conference followed just a few days later. It passed a resolution on giving out birth control information with a large majority. Of course this was just one issue among many discussed; indeed it was only one part of a resolution about maternity. This was perhaps Dorothy's happiest moment in politics: debating the issues she really cared about with a sympathetic audience and a real hope that something might be done. It is no wonder that, perhaps recalling the 'entertainments' of her suffragette days, she burst into song, adapting an American strikers' song for the occasion:

> As we come marching, we bring the Greater Days
> The rising of Women means the rising of the race
> No more the drudge and the idler, ten that toil where one reposes
> But a sharing of life's glories; Bread and Roses; Bread and Roses.[32]

After the Conference, Dorothy joined with Dora Russell to form the Workers' Birth

IN PARLIAMENT 59

Control Group; Susan Lawrence was also involved. Dora later was generous in her praise of Dorothy's work in this field: 'as a single woman she showed courage in dealing with a topic then so shocking as sex'.³³ Their aim was to make it possible for working women to get birth control information and treatment, safely and without charge. The issue came before Parliament on 30 July. Wheatley was asked if he would consider allowing local authorities to give out information about methods of birth control without penalising these authorities by taking away their maternity and child welfare grants. It was pointed out that a conference of Labour women had recently voted for this.

Dorothy asked Wheatley a question too:

> *Is the Minister aware that many working-class women attending these welfare centres are unfit to bear children and to bring up healthy children, and the doctors know they are unfit, and yet they are unable to give this information, which any upper or middle-class woman can obtain from a private doctor; and will he consider the bearing of this on abortion, which is so terribly on the increase in this country?*

(By 'unfit', Dorothy clearly meant simply medically unfit. A change in the sense of the word since has given a remark almost a 'Nazi' flavour: there was no-one more opposed to the racist ideas of the Nazis and similar groups than Dorothy Jewson.)

Wheatley was put in a difficult position by these questions. As a radical Minister of Health he might have been expected to offer his support, but as a practising Roman Catholic he could not agree with birth control. He replied rather vaguely that these were topics that could perhaps be raised before Parliament, but that for the moment he was just carrying out his instructions.

This was not the only setback for Dorothy and people who shared her radical views. By the summer of 1924, many people felt that the first ever Labour Government had been a disappointment. It had failed to bring in any radical reforms: of course it could only put through measures that another party would support. Radical women, especially, felt that they had been let down. *Time and Tide* talked of non-party women 'who, full of hope at the achievement of a new Government deeply pledged on questions which they had at heart, are growing daily more annoyed and perturbed at the Government's entire oblivion of past promises'.³⁴

In July, Dorothy spoke in a debate on setting up agricultural wages committees:

> *I think it is very important to realise in this Debate that this is not only a rural question affecting the agricultural workers, but is also a question which concerns those hon. Members who represent urban constituencies. For my part, representing Norwich, I can say that the problem of the agricultural*

> worker is constantly with us. During the last 50 or 60 years, thousands of workers have been driven from the land and have had to seek refuge in Norwich. Very badly paid and unskilled work has been found for them, and factories have been started which have absorbed this lowly-paid labour. The question of the position of the agricultural worker in Norfolk is, therefore, a vital one and I welcome any Measure, even this Bill as it stands after the Committee stage, which will give those workers some sort of machinery to help them to improve the conditions under which they live. Everyone will agree that the present position is chaotic. The conciliation committees have been absolutely useless, and the wages of the workers are a disgrace to a civilised country.

In the following month, she raised another favourite concern of hers, conditions for women in the catering trade. She urged Margaret Bondfield, as the Government minister responsible, to apply the Trades Boards Acts to this group of workers: the minister agreed that this should be looked into. In the same month, Dorothy combined with a Tory female MP, Lady Astor, to raise another issue that was important to her – the question of equal pay for male and female government workers. She asked the Chancellor of the Exchequer, William Graham, to set up a Committee to discuss this question. Graham referred to a reply made by his predecessor, Philip Snowden, to Lady Astor on 3 July: he had said that the question would be reviewed within three years; Lady Astor had retorted that this was shameful in view of Labour party pledges at the election. Snowden said that he knew of no such pledges, and that Astor was very well informed about labour policies; she retorted 'I have had to fight against them and I know'. Now, on 6 August, Dorothy asked if this reply was not contrary 'to the spirit, if not the letter, of the Sex Disqualification Removal Act'. Astor once more intervened: 'Does not the Hon Gentleman think it was contrary to the election promises of the Labour party?' In fact Nancy Astor was quite right: the Labour Party manifesto at the 1923 election said:

> Labour stands for equality between men and women: equal political and legal rights, equal rights and privileges in parenthood, equal pay for equal work.[35]

Graham gave the classic response of 'reforming' governments – they had decided that they could not afford to make the change because of the enormous expense that would be involved.

During the summer recess, Dorothy was able to visit Russia: she went with twenty other labour leaders on a trip organised by the Workers' Travel Association. They arrived at Leningrad and then travelled to Moscow, their prime purpose being to study Soviet educational methods. She said that the Russians received them with open arms as the first contingent of workers to visit the Soviet Republic. While the rest of the group travelled down the Volga she stayed on in Moscow, even attending a plenary session of the Moscow Soviet. She also visited factories, schools and new workers' houses and attended a meeting of delegated women factory workers at which she gave a speech. Labour politicians tended to look at Russia with rose-tinted glasses, as it was in a sense the first country run by and for the working class: Dorothy seem to have been less smitten than Susan Lawrence, who, after her visit, put a Soviet flag on the wall of her flat and started addressing people as 'comrade'![36]

Dorothy was especially interested as the Jewson family already had dealings with Soviet Russia in connection with the timber trade: they had traded with Tsarist Russia before the First World War. In 1921, they became the first English company to have a contract with the Russian government after the Revolution, and in November 1923 they announced a deal to buy up all the timber in Petrograd that was ready for shipping, some 22,000 trees worth between £300,000 and £400,000.

During her time as an MP, she was also able to provide direct help for at least one of her constituents, a Norwich woman whose husband had died in the war but who had been unable to obtain a war pension. Dorothy intervened personally with the Minister for Pensions, and, although rebuffed at first, she was eventually successful. There were dark mutterings on the local Pension Committee about political collusion, but, as was pointed out at the time, the important thing was the result: the woman now had her pension.

The main achievement of the first-ever Labour government was Wheatley's Housing Act which enabled local authorities to build many more houses which the working class could afford to rent. MacDonald himself was mainly interested in foreign affairs, including attempts to come to an agreement with Soviet Russia; the Government would probably have been defeated over this issue if it came to a vote as the opposition parties were against it. However, they were defeated before this over a lesser issue involving attempts to suppress the writings of a Communist journalist, J. R. Campbell. Conservatives and Liberals alike voted against the government, which fell after just ten months in power: in October 1924 a general election was called for the third year in a row.

In the summer of 1924, Baldwin changed his mind once again on Protection. Most Liberal voters were committed to free trade as one of their cardinal principles, so Baldwin's change of heart meant that they might be tempted to vote for him, especially if he was able to portray the battle at the next election as being a straightforward struggle against Socialism. As soon as the election was announced, it became clear that the Liberals and Conservatives in Norwich were plotting to work together against the sitting Labour MPs. Neither Roberts nor Swan stood and the Conservative put

Two images of Dorothy during the 1924 campaign, one taken from the joint manifesto she issued with Walter Smith.

DOROTHY JEWSON, B.A.

W. R. SMITH.

up just one candidate, Captain Griffyth Fairfax, a barrister who stressed his military connections by appearing in uniform in his nomination photograph. The Liberals stuck with Hilton Young, their former MP. He had married Kathleen Scott, widow of the Antarctic explorer, in 1922, their son Wayland being born the following year. Now he was able to proclaim family values by showing photographs of Kathleen and Wayland: he said that he had been watching him play with a box of bricks. Wayland did not know how to make anything out of them and left them all 'higgledy-piggledy' – to laughter, Young said this put him in mind of the record of the Socialist government.

Dorothy and Smith issued a joint manifesto. Inevitably this had to praise the work of the Labour Government: 'the record of the Labour Government during its brief term of office is one that must command the confidence of all who wish to see social well-being at home, and peace and goodwill among the Nations abroad'. This line was especially difficult for Dorothy as she did not support many of its actions, considering them insufficiently radical. The manifesto did include one dangerously radical section, that on unemployment: 'it is well to emphasise once again that no final solution can be found within the existing order. It is part of the Capitalist system of society, and will only be removed when that system can be replaced by one based upon co-operation and social service'.

The election was once more a rowdy one with Labour supporters heckling Young and Fairfax – police had to be called to a Fairfax meeting at Angel Road School on 16 October. It was at this meeting that Fairfax said that although Smith was a worker, Dorothy was a capitalist. When it was pointed out that she was actually a trade union worker, Fairfax retorted that she was living off inherited money, having been left several thousand pounds by a relative – 'he took it that she was a capitalist': Fairfax was referring to the inheritance left to Dorothy by her father. Clearly this shows that she came from a very different world from most Labour supporters, but it seems unfair to criticise a woman for receiving a bequest from her own father. Fairfax himself seems to have realised he had gone too far: at a later meeting he conceded that, rich or poor, she was entitled to represent any party in whose policy she sincerely believed.

Jewson family affairs continued to dog the election campaign. On 21 October, Dorothy's uncle, Richard Jewson, spoke in favour of Hilton Young who, he claimed to some laughter and applause, 'was the greatest statesman who had ever fought their battles and represented them in Parliament '. He specifically told his listeners to vote for Young and Fairfax. He claimed that he knew about Russia from his experiences in the timber business. On the following day, Dorothy's brother Christopher spoke in favour of Dorothy and questioned Richard's knowledge. Relations with Russia were an important topic: the 'Red Scare' was a factor in the election. A letter, allegedly by Zinoviev, President of the Communist International, was published during the election campaign itself. It implied that that there was an international conspiracy to spread Bolshevik Communism. A heckler at one meeting asked Dorothy if she received orders from Moscow. To laughter and applause, she replied 'I haven't had any instructions from Moscow. Of course it is just a lie to mislead you'.

A week before the election, Dorothy talked about the role of women, claiming that Fairfax did not want to extend the vote to women without a property qualification. Dorothy said nearly five million women had not got the vote on the same terms as men – they were mainly women of the working classes – she contended that it was women of the working classes who most needed the vote (applause). 'What had property to do with it? Teachers, nurses and many other women lived in rooms, and because they did not possess furniture they were disenfranchised. What did it matter what furniture they possessed? Women would play a more important role in this election than any in the past (applause)'. Dorothy spoke from personal experience: as an unmarried woman living in her mother's home, she was not entitled to vote in the election![37]

A letter from 'Progress' published in the local press commented: 'I cannot for the life of me understand any Liberal voting for the Conservatives at the coming election … my second vote is going to the Labour Party, whose aims are an extension of Liberal principles, and I venture, sir I am not alone'. This was an appeal to return to the 1906-1911 situation where Liberal and Labour combined against the Conservatives. However, times had changed as the result showed:

1924 GENERAL ELECTION

Hilton Young (Liberal)	28,842
Griffyth Fairfax (Conservative)	28,529
W. R. Smith (Labour)	23,808
D. Jewson (Labour)	22,931

The Conservative/Liberal alliance had paid off: no less than 27,131 voted for both Young and Fairfax. As *The Times* pointed out, this was a surprise. It had been thought that many Liberals in Norwich would stick to the guiding principle of their forefathers – 'Always vote against a Tory when you see one'. Only 900 people took the advice of 'Progress' and voted for Young and one of the Labour candidates. Just 167 people 'plumped' for Dorothy – Fairfax had almost a thousand plumpers behind him.

In the country as a whole, the Labour vote actually rose by about one million. However, this was swamped by a mass desertion of the Liberal party by the voters, mainly in favour of the Conservatives. After the election the Conservatives had an enormous majority, with 419 MPs. The number of Labour MPs fell by 40 to 151, but it was the Liberals who were the clear losers: they were left with just 40 MPs. Baldwin was back, but the Labour Party was now clearly established as the main opposition party.

Was Dorothy simply defeated by a general swing against Labour, or was it something more personal? Martin Francis wrote that 'support for local authority provision of family planning advice contributed to Dorothy Jewson losing her Norwich seat in 1924', and Labour historian Martin Pugh echoes this opinion. Baroness Hollis, with her unique knowledge of the Norwich political scene, thought the same: 'Because she fought to get birth control advice to married women whose health was being destroyed by relentless pregnancies, she in turn was destroyed by the Norwich clergy who campaigned ruthlessly to ensure she lost her seat'. However, her vote in the two elections remained constant at 800 to 900 behind that of Walter Smith, who was not tarred with association with this contentious issue.[38]

The Liberal-supporting *Eastern Daily Press* was naturally triumphant, suggesting that the Labour members had lost because they had not been sufficiently radical – the red corpuscles in their blood had turned out to be pink! This might have been true of the Labour Government in general, and of Walter Smith, whose youthful radicalism seems to have faded. It was completely untrue of Dorothy, whose willingness to speak out may have her cost her in the long run. She was the one female MP to take up specifically feminist issues: Martin Pugh calls her 'the woman who took most risks' while Stella Browne praised Dorothy's 'passionate sympathy and loyalty, strategic breadth of vision, utter contempt for self-advertisement and advantage'.[39]

Dorothy's friends and Labour Party colleagues, Margaret Bondfield and Susan Lawrence, were also defeated in the 1924 election. This was not the end of their careers, however. Margaret Bondfield was re-elected in 1926 and in 1929 became Minister of Labour in Ramsay MacDonald's second Labour government, thus becoming the first woman Cabinet minister in British history. Susan Lawrence was back in Parliament in 1929 and was appointed Parliamentary Secretary to the Minister of Health. If Dorothy had got back into Parliament, she would probably have achieved high Government office. Baroness Hollis has commented 'she had more warmth than Susan Lawrence and more ability and courage . . . than Margaret Bondfield'.[40]

For Dorothy there was to be no return to Westminster. However, she was now seen as an internationally-minded feminist and socialist. Her most explicit comments about her ten months in Parliament were made – in German – in an Austrian radical feminist publication, *Die Frau*, while she was still an MP. She wrote that what struck her most about Parliament was the terrible waste of time and the lack of any sense of the importance of a matter. Both Houses were overloaded with a tradition of heritage, habit and ancient customs. She also painted a dismal picture of social conditions in her home city, describing housing in Norwich as a disgrace to civilisation: when campaigning she had come across many houses that were completely unsuitable for human occupation.

These twin themes of internationalism and local social issues were to be Dorothy's main concerns for the rest of her career.

7

Leading from the left
1924–37

Baldwin's Conservative government was a quiet one, without any major reforms. The greatest achievement of the government was to introduce full democracy to Britain: an Act of 1928 allowed women to vote on equal terms with men. At last one of Dorothy's main political objectives had been achieved: now it was time to work for social change for men and women alike.

Although no longer MPs, Dorothy and Smith were still influential in Norwich, as the Labour candidates in the next election, whenever it might come. Dorothy had a wide range of political interests, all concerned either with family matters or with pacifism. She became a member of the Children's Committee at the Law Courts, set up to consider changes to the Children's Act, and was the only woman on a committee set up to consider the question of legal aid to the poor. Typically, she and one other committee member (Rhys Davies) produced a minority report proposing more radical solutions than the report by the majority. The main report suggested a voluntary system while Dorothy and Davies wanted the local authority to provide legal aid.

Dorothy continued to take a stand on the birth control issue. She spoke in March 1925 to a conference of the National Union of Societies for Equal Citizenship, which was the successor body to the NUWSS. She proposed a motion calling on the Ministry of Health to allow information on methods of birth control to be given by medical officers at maternity and child welfare clinics: however, she, like many other Labour women, left this organisation over the next few years as its support dwindled: it came to an end when equal suffrage had finally been achieved.

The issue came to a head at successive Labour Party conferences, in 1925 and 1926. In 1926, Dorothy, together with Dora Russell, tried to commit the Labour Party to the establishment of welfare centres to provide free birth-control information. The ILP passed a resolution to this effect almost unanimously but they could not get it agreed to at the Labour Party Conference. Dorothy thought the defeat showed the Labour Party's disregard for women: 'if there had been as good a representation of mothers as there was of fathers, there is no doubt what the verdict would have been, for there is no subject on which women feel with such passionate emotions at the present time'.

The 1926 Conference was held at Margate Winter Gardens. Dorothy and Dora had to stand on chairs to speak: 'two contrasting heads and voices – hazel brown and clearly chiselled treble, silvery black and resonant mezzo – focussed attention'. They did win the right to further discussion by a very close margin – 1,656,000 votes in favour, to 1,620,000 against – but nothing happened. At the following Party Conference, Ramsay MacDonald spoke against it: he did not wish to alienate Roman Catholics. However, Dorothy and her friends had sown the seeds. In 1930, another Labour Minister of Health allowed maternity clinics to give information and advice on birth control 'in case of medical necessity', and some local authorities, mainly London boroughs, began to do this. The Workers' Birth Control Group had achieved its object: Pamela Graves calls it 'an outstanding example of a single issue lobbying organisation'.[41]

The General Strike

The year 1926 was dominated by the General Strike. This arose from the crisis in the coal-mining industry: the owners of the mines wanted to make the miners work even longer hours than they were already doing – and for less money. On 1 May 1926 they were locked out of the mines. The TUC responded by calling a general strike to start on 3 May. In 1924, the *Eastern Daily Press* had described Smith as 'the last person in the world to man a barricade', but he and Dorothy rose to the occasion: both were experienced trade union organisers, of course.

Norwich Labour Party held a rally in the Market Place every year on the Sunday nearest to May Day. In 1926 the rally was held on 2 May: Smith and Dorothy were there, and Dorothy spoke in support of the miners:

> A call had come from every mining village to the workers of the community. The mining industry was not the only one that was breaking down under the capitalist system. The agricultural industry was in the same position and all over Norfolk there were men working for a wage of 30 shillings. The same was true for other industries . . . The solution of the Labour Party to the problem was the socialisation of the mining industry [Cheers] and the

> *only solution of unemployment was public ownership in the interest of the community and run by the community.*

A report of activities in Norwich in the general strike said, that as well as a Strike Committee sitting 24 hours a day (in relays) and an Advisory Committee meeting every night, a Committee had been formed to arrange meetings of all kinds, including public meetings on street corners and in public halls:

> W. R. Smith and Dorothy Jewson the Parl[iamentary] cand[idate]s are on the committee and have been useful in using their influence. The Chief Constable in the interests of order has granted the use of Public Halls and Parks for meeting and recreation purposes. The City Football Club has also lent its grounds. The relation between ourselves and the police is of a most amiable character.
> The number at present engaged is approximately 4,500.
> It is supposed that next week there will be (owing to the indirect operations of the strike such as the overstocking of factories) 10,000 out.[42]

In fact the Liberal MP Herbert Samuel drew up compromise proposals for the miners and the General Strike was called off after nine days. However neither the miners nor the owners would accept the report. The miners held out for six months until they were starving. They had to accept everything the strike had been against, longer hours and lower wages. Norwich Labour Party held a carnival every year in Earlham Park. The carnival in July 1926 was held after the General Strike was over, but while the miners were still on strike. Over 15,000 people came to hear the main speaker, George Lansbury; George Edwards of the Agricultural Workers' Union and Walter Smith were also on the platform. Dorothy was President; she brought three miners' lamps onto the stage and these were raffled in aid of the strikers' relief fund.

Labour Party rally at Earlham Park; from right to left George Lansbury (speaking); Walter Smith; George Edwards; Dorothy Jewson; unidentified woman

Smith took advantage of the carnival's

surroundings. He pointed out that Earlham Park had been bought by the city council for the benefit of the people of Norwich. The council had also taken the provision of houses out of the hands of individuals: he looked forward to a time when the main industries in the country would be dealt with in the same way.[43]

Out of Parliament, Dorothy undoubtedly felt frustrated by the lack of radicalism within the Labour Party. As a result, she became increasingly identified with the ILP: she was a member of its National Administrative Council from 1925 to 1934. She now devoted her energies to a new issue, family endowment, later better known as family or children's allowance. She wrote a short leaflet published by the ILP in 1926 which was sold at meetings for one penny, and whose title summed up her concerns: *Socialists and the Family: a plea for family endowment'*. This looked at the issue of child and family poverty:

> *Whether under Capitalism or Socialism, we must face up to the injustice of providing for the family through the wage of an individual, based altogether on his earning powers and with no consideration for his domestic circumstances. This method is unfair to the children, unfair to the mother, and contrary to our principle of giving 'each according to his need' ... We believe mothers and children have a right to a SHARE OF THEIR OWN in the wealth of the community.*

She urged a universal grant out of public funds, the amount depending upon the number of children in the family. She calculated that to pay five shillings a week for every child under fifteen would cost £158 million, commenting, in true Socialist style: 'a Government that can spend 120 million on armaments and three hundred million on War Debt can surely spend this on its children'.[44]

She was clear that both mother and child would gain: 'the working class mother sees in children's allowances a means of using her new political power to save her children from the worst effects of a vicious system. For herself, she will gain some recognition from the State of the value of her work in rearing children, and the increased independence that will come from greater security.'

Dorothy spoke in favour of a family allowance at several Party Conferences, but unfortunately, although the ILP was in favour, the Labour Party was divided: many union leaders thought that if families received the allowance from the State, then employers would seize on it as an excuse to cut wages. Unlike her campaign for birth control information, her struggle for family allowances was unsuccessful.

Meanwhile, there had been great changes in Dorothy's political and personal life. She was elected for Norwich City council in November 1927: this aspect of her career is considered in the next chapter. In 1928, she moved out of Tower House and set up home with Maud at Wensum Cottage, 53, Lower Road, Hellesdon, next door to her brother Christopher's house, Riverdene. Christopher and his wife Annie had moved to Hellesdon in 1919: the properties took water from a well in the grounds, which was still in use in the 1960s.[45]

In April 1928, the Independent Labour Party National Conference was held in Norwich for the first time since 1915. This time, however, it was a triumph, and one in which Dorothy fully shared; she was on the executive council as one of nine divisional representatives. There were over 400 delegates at the opening meeting at St Andrew's Hall on 7 April: Dorothy was on the podium. She proposed creating an ILP Women's Group National Advisory Committee and this was agreed. On the following day there was an evening meeting at the Haymarket Picture Palace. Dorothy presided over the meeting and drew attention to the success of the Labour Party in the city: ten years earlier there had only been eight Labour representatives on public bodies in the city, now there were 25 on the City Council and 23 on the Board of Guardians. The Lord Mayor in 1927–28 was Herbert Witard, the first Labour politician to achieve this honour.

Historian David Howell sums up Dorothy at this time: 'A member of a prominent Norwich family, a suffragist and pacifist, she combined vigorous campaigning on women's issues with general support of the ILP's radicalization.' In fact the ILP was becoming very much a left-wing pressure group. Leading Labour politicians were resigning from it, Margaret Bondfield and Philip Snowden, both in the 1920s, and Ramsay MacDonald himself in 1930. Dorothy stayed and was one of the leading figures within the group – she was even nominated to be Party Chairman in 1929 and 1931 but did not win sufficient support on either occasion.[46]

Dorothy was also very active in the Women's Group within the Labour Party. The first Conference of Women after the fall of the Labour government took place in May 1925 in Birmingham: there were between 900 and a thousand delegates – including all three former MPs – but they could only debate and pass resolutions. At the 1928 Women's Conference, Dorothy moved resolutions demanding the right of the conference to put forward three resolutions at the Party Conference, and to elect the women members on the National Executive directly, but this was not accepted by the full Party Conference. In 1931 she tried to obtain an independent role in policy-making for the Women's Conference. These resolutions were all being passed by the women but not even debated by the full Party Conference. A substantial minority of women were beginning to question if it was worthwhile to have a separate conference at all, but Dorothy was not among them: she wanted to keep the Women's Conference and give it more teeth.

Another issue with which Dorothy became closely associated was that of laws protecting women workers: she wanted future employment laws to be based on the job itself rather than the gender of the worker. Once again she was in the same camp as Dora Russell, and once again she was taking a different line to the Labour Party, which favoured protective laws specifically aimed at women: in 1929, former colleague Marion Phillips openly rebuked Dorothy for her failure to toe the party line: her relations with old colleagues in the movement were becoming increasingly strained.

Dorothy remained a pacifist, and was a supporter of international socialism. She was an active member of the No More War Committee, and in August 1925 was one of the British delegates at the International Conference of Labour and Socialist Women in Marseilles in France: other delegates included Marion Phillips and Margaret Bondfield. She explained why she thought these conferences were important when she attended an International Socialist Conference in 1926: she valued 'the rubbing shoulders together, the sympathy and better understanding . . . linking all nations in the Socialist faith'. In 1927 she became one of three British women on the International Advisory Committee and she was present at their first conference held in Brussels in August 1928: 95 delegates turned up representing 16 countries. Here she was representing the ILP rather than the Labour Party, and she clashed with them for not wanting to raise the birth control issue: she mocked another former friend, Susan Lawrence, for saying, 'if they had known it would be raised, I doubt if our own men would have let us come'. Dorothy was moving away from her more orthodox associates in the party, and moving to the left even of the ILP. In 1927, the latter debated whether to affiliate to the League Against Imperialism, a truly international organisation. The ILP decided against as the organisation could be seen as a communist front: Dorothy was one of the few to speak in favour of affiliation.[47]

The 1929 general election

The Conservative Government ran its full term of five years. Finally Baldwin called an election to be held in May 1929. This was an election fought between three great leaders, all of whom had at one time been Prime Minister: Baldwin for the Conservatives, MacDonald for Labour, and Lloyd George for the Liberals. It was also the first in which everyone over the age of 21 could vote. This meant that women were in the majority in the electorate: in Norwich there were 44,987 women who could vote compared with 37,156 men. However there were still very few women candidates. Dorothy was one of them: she and Smith stood once more for Labour. Again the Liberals and Conservatives put up just a single candidate: the Conservatives chose Griffith Fairfax once more, the Liberals Geoffrey Shakespeare, a London journalist. Shakespeare was a Norwich man: his father had been preacher at St Mary's Baptist Chapel, the church at which the Jewson family worshipped.

The 1929 election: Dorothy, Walter Smith, female supporters.

The campaign involved the usual meetings, held mainly in local schools. On 22 May, Dorothy said that, as the Liberals had no hope of forming a government, a vote for them was in effect a vote for the Conservatives. On the following day, speaking at Bull Close Road School, she addressed social issues. She said that the Tories were claiming to have built 900,000 houses during their five years in power. In fact 220,000 of these had been built under the Wheatley Act introduced by the previous Labour administration. These were houses built to let, and the only ones that the working classes could afford. Most of the other houses were larger and intended for owner occupiers. She was applauded when she declared her readiness to tax the rich: '[Labour] believed that the money spent on luxury and preparations for the same should be spent by the workers who produced the wealth.'

All four candidates spoke at a women-only meeting at the Agricultural Hall in Norwich on 23 May; no men were present apart from a few stewards and the candidates themselves. Each candidate spoke briefly and then fielded questions. Dorothy joked that this year the election result lay not so much in the lap of the gods as of the goddesses, as women were now in the majority. Inevitably the issue of her personal fortune was raised, one woman asking whether she would adopt practical socialism by sharing her wealth. Dorothy retorted that she would share with other women if she thought it would help and that she was already doing that to a great extent. This drew applause: her personal generosity was well known. She went on: 'I believe the honest way to advance other women in any position is to come into the Socialist movement and give what time and money I possess fighting the system that makes slums, bad housing, low wages and unemployment. These are the things we are fighting in the Labour movement and I believe it is the best way in which we can deal with them'.

At the end of the campaign both Labour and the Conservatives attacked the Liberal party. At a meeting at St Andrew's Hall on 27 May Dorothy said: 'James Henry Tillett and the early Liberals would turn in their graves if they knew that the

The 1929 election: the candidates

Liberals of the present day were adopting that policy [of giving their second vote to the Conservatives]. A heckler at a Conservative meeting was blunter: 'the only Liberals you can trust are in the Rosary'. If Dorothy heard this it must have struck home: many of her Liberal Party ancestors were buried in the Rosary, which was a Norwich cemetery favoured by Nonconformist families.[48]

GENERAL ELECTION 1929

G. Shakespeare (Lib)	33,974
W. R. Smith (Lab)	33,690
D. Jewson (Lab)	31,040
G. Fairfax (Con)	30,793

The split *The Times* had predicted in 1923 had finally come about, with one Labour and one Liberal candidate being elected. It was the plumpers and cross-voters who swung the scale against Dorothy. No less than 30,028 people had voted for both Smith and Jewson, compared with just 27,470 voting for the Shakespeare/Fairfax combination. However, Shakespeare received the votes of 3,123 plumpers, and Fairfax those of 2,876: Dorothy only got 28. No less than 2,846 people cast one vote for the Shakespeare and one for Smith, only 535 for Shakespeare and Dorothy. These small groups of voters cost Dorothy her chance of re-election.

This time, Dorothy had polled over 2,500 votes less than her colleague Walter Smith. Perhaps her continued work on the birth control issue was in people's minds, or perhaps her ideas were simply becoming too left wing for some voters. Her Christian pacifism may have had an effect: at the women's meeting already mentioned she had been happy to agree that a Labour Government would abolish the armed forces, and even the police force. This fearless honesty, which earned her the name 'Our Dorothy', was in contrast to Smith, whose unwillingness to commit himself to unpopular policies led to his nickname of 'wily Walter'.

Dorothy was to stand just once more, and then under very different circumstances.[49]

The second Labour Government

Labour almost doubled their representation in the new Parliament, with 288 seats. The Conservatives fell to 260 seats: for the first time ever, Labour was the largest party. Ramsay MacDonald formed his second government but once again it was a minority one: Conservatives and Liberals could combine together to defeat him. It failed to introduce any socialist measures, and the ILP members within it became restless.

Dorothy spoke at the 1929 Labour Party conference, held at Brighton in October, putting forward a motion in favour of family allowances. Her themes were familiar — she wanted great increases in taxes on the wealthy to fund social services, in particular an effective system of children's allowances. Princes and Princesses had allowances for births, she said, so she saw no reason why everyone else did not. J. R. Clynes (as Home Secretary) replied that the executive sympathised with her views, but the trades unions remained divided on the question.

In fact the Government was almost at once overwhelmed by economic crisis. The 'Great Depression' had begun in America in October 1929. In England there was a massive rise in unemployment: there were 2 million unemployed in July 1930 and 2.5 million by December. MacDonald wanted to save money by cutting state benefits: Dorothy, of course, fiercely opposed this from outside Parliament but her former colleague Margaret Bondfield, in MacDonald's Cabinet as Minister of Labour, was prepared to support the proposal. However, nine other Cabinet ministers were opposed. MacDonald discussed the crisis with other party leaders and they agreed to form a National Government of all three parties, with MacDonald continuing as Prime Minister. However, only sixteen Labour MPs supported the new Government: the remainder of the 280 odd Labour MPs, including Walter Smith, moved onto the Opposition benches. The government passed an emergency budget in September, reducing by 10% the wages of everyone paid by the State, from cabinet ministers to the unemployed. Almost every Labour MP voted against the budget, but it was carried by a majority of 50. In October, MacDonald called a general election as a vote of confidence in his government: he asked for 'a doctor's mandate'.

The 1931 election saw two candidates in Norwich who supported the National Government: the Liberal Geoffrey Shakespeare and the Conservative George Hartland, who replaced Fairfax. The Labour Party was split: disputes between the official Party and the ILP were reaching breaking point. The Labour Party was actually holding its annual conference in Scarborough when the election was announced. It tightened up its constitution, only being willing to support candidates who would promise to be loyal to the Party once they were in Parliament. The ILP leader, Fenner Brockway, said that 14 of the ILP MPs would decline to accept these Standing Orders, and a small number of other candidates were also loyal to the ILP. Dorothy was one of this tiny group, and this meant that she could not stand as an official Labour candidate in the election, but only as a candidate for the ILP. Smith, who had now moved decisively to the right, did not want an ILP stable-mate and showed 'considerable hostility': he wanted Fred Jex as an orthodox Labour Party running partner, and threatened not to stand otherwise: however, the ILP stood firm and Smith had to make the best of the situation.[50]

The *Eastern Daily Press* summed up the situation:

> *Once again Labour is to be represented at the election by Mr W. R. Smith and Miss Dorothy Jewson, but this time with a difference. Only the former has the full and unquestioned support of the Norwich Labour party, the latter, staunchly upholding the policies and the creed of the ILP, can have only the 'moral' support of the official party since the Scarborough Conference decreed it that the party label could only be borne by those who pledge themselves both to talk and to walk in the House of Commons as they are told by the party executive. In debate and division alike the decree of the executive is to be paramount. So, during the election the Labour platform will be occupied only by Mr Smith: Miss Jewson — unless she is to put him in jeopardy of expulsion by his party — must fight her own hand as the candidate of a group.*[51]

There was a bizarre adoption meeting at Bull Close Road School on 15 October. The two candidates stood on separate platforms to be nominated by their respective groups of supporters. On the same evening Dorothy spoke at Angel Road School. She was scathing about the new government formed by her old party boss, MacDonald:

> *The Socialist movement has anticipated this crisis for a long time. Today we are facing not merely the break-up of the industrial world, but the break-up of our financial system, which is after all the very essence of Capitalism — a crisis as serious as ever faced in this country. In the face of that crisis the National Government — what a mockery, because it was National in no sense of the word — was led by Mr Ramsay MacDonald, a deserter from our ranks and once the most hated man by the Tories, but who is now described as 'the most noble saviour the country has ever had'. And why? Because he had listened to the dictates of the city; because he had given way to the dictates of the money-lenders and money barons who controlled our finance, and whose advice Mr Lloyd George had said was generally wrong.*[52]

Freedom from an official party line gave Dorothy free vein to put forward radical views. On 20 October, speaking at the Avenue Road school, she called for a National Investment Board:

> *If you are going to allow the bankers to be the masters of the industry then this country can only go down the hill and we are going to see a national crisis compared to which the present crisis is a mere nothing. This country will go down in confusion and chaos, and bloodshed, and possibly war.*

Three nights later, speaking at Horn's Lane school, she was calmer:

1931 election candidates

Next day she was going to the Nest to support Norwich City in their football match, but what concerned her much more was what Norwich City was to do on Thursday. It did not concern her so much as it did the citizens generally. Her policy was one that would benefit all the people in the country and particularly the working classes who had suffered so much.

On the following day she did go to the Nest. A record league attendance — over 17,000 — saw Norwich play Southend, who were the only unbeaten team in the League. The result of the match was a respectable 1-1 draw, but, when polling day came, that result was less satisfactory.

1931 GENERAL ELECTION

G. Shakespeare (National Liberal)	40,925
G. Hartland (National Conservative)	38,883
W. Smith (Labour)	28,295
D. Jewson (Labour, nominated by ILP)	26,537

The two supporters of MacDonald's coalition each polled over 10,000 more votes than the two Labour candidates. 'Wily Walter' obtained about 2,000 more votes more than Dorothy: again he was the more popular of the two. No doubt, Dorothy anticipated the result. The local press reported that, at 2.30 am on the morning of the counting of the votes at St Andrew's Hall, 'Miss Jewson walked across the Plain, a lone figure. There was no demonstration, except that one woman rushed up and shook her by the hand'.[53]

In reality, her 26,537 votes were a great personal success considering the unpopularity of the Labour Party as a whole at this election. Indeed by the evening she had recovered her spirits, telling a meeting at the Keir Hardie Hall 'how much she had appreciated the work done on her behalf: in fact she had been the happiest

Declaring the 1931 election result outside Norwich's Guildhall. Dorothy is second from the left.

candidate in the country'. A supporter shouted 'Good old Dorothy' and the Hall erupted with applause.

The National Government obtained the largest majority ever recorded in British politics: it received over 60% of the votes and won 521 seats. Labour's vote fell by only two million, but in terms of seats the election was a disaster. Every former cabinet minister was defeated and the party returned just 52 MPs. All its women MPs, including Margaret Bondfield, Susan Lawrence and Marion Phillips (who had been elected in 1929) were swept away. In the 1929–31 Parliament, 142 Labour MPs had been members of the ILP. In 1931 there were just 19 ILP candidates not endorsed by the Labour party, including Dorothy in Norwich. Only three were elected, all from Glasgow (two other ILP supporters, also from Scottish constituencies, were elected under trades union auspices). In the new Parliament, the Speaker recognised the ILP as a separate political party.[54]

At their 1932 Easter Conference, the ILP debated whether to leave the Labour Party but decided to remain within it on their own terms. However, the Labour Party conference that year decided to disaffiliate the ILP: the ILP held a special conference and voted to leave the Labour Party because of its failure to commit itself to Socialism.

The great majority of former ILP members now deserted it, so that they could remain part of the official Labour Party. However, a very small number of people decided to risk their political careers by committing themselves to the ILP cause; Dorothy was one. She wrote to the secretary of the Labour Group on Norwich City Council explaining that she had decided to break with the group and to contest her seat as an ILP candidate. She was forthright in explaining the background to her decision. She said that, during her eight months in Parliament, the ILP had been in continual conflict with the Labour Government and that she 'was compelled to vote against the Labour Government unless I was to dishonour my election pledges or oppose Labour Party Conference decisions. Members of the ILP were then free to vote independently and this right had been frequently exercised by Philip Snowden and others in the past, and never been challenged'.

By the time of the 1929 Labour Government, she said, the Standing Rules of the Labour Party had changed: MPs were now forbidden to vote contrary to instructions. She claimed that this Government had made 'direct attacks' on working class people. As examples she referred to the Unemployment Insurance Bill, the Anomalies Act – which, she claimed, deprived 180,000 workers of unemployment benefit – and the setting up of the May Committee 'by whose recommendations the means test is now being carried out with such inhuman cruelty'.[55]

The decision to leave the Labour Party and stay with the ILP meant the end of Dorothy's alliance with Margaret Bondfield and Susan Lawrence, both of whom remained with the Labour Party (Bondfield had left the ILP many years earlier).

Her only allies now were in the small group of people who also felt they could no longer work within the Labour Party, including James Maxton, Fenner Brockway and Campbell Stephen. The number of members of the ILP declined rapidly after the split, from about 17,000 in 1931 to 4,000 in 1935.[56]

As one of only two female ex-MPs in their ranks, Dorothy was one of the leading figures within the much-reduced ILP (the other was Jennie Lee, who, unlike Dorothy, was to return to the Labour Party and to Parliament). She remained on the executive council for another two years, until the Easter 1934 Conference when she was voted off, to be replaced as the representative for East Anglia by her Norwich comrade, George F. Johnson, a councillor and former metalwork instructor at the Technical Institute in Norwich.

Norwich was, in fact, one of the few strongholds of the Independent Labour Party. Matthew Worley comments that the city had 'one of the most active and well-supported branches of the ILP — one of the few constituencies where the ILP retained an influence after it had disaffiliated from the Labour Party'. The ILP had the great advantage of possession — it was they who owned the Keir Hardie Memorial Hall. It continued to be used for the social events so important to a group like the ILP — whist drives, jumble sales and dances. Sometimes Dorothy would speak at these gatherings of the faithful. The official Labour Party had to find new premises, buying Brunswick Lodge on Newmarket Road and, in 1935, 59 Bethel Street.[57]

Many years later Len Stevenson, a member, was to recall that 'it was just Glasgow, Bradford and Norwich were the people who stuck with the ILP'. In Norwich, Witard and Smith went with the official Labour Party, as did Fred Jex, who was Lord Mayor in 1933–34: this prize was attainable by Labour Party councillors, but not by those, like Dorothy, who had committed themselves to the ILP. The ILP membership in Norwich was about 450 before the split: in most other areas the membership then plummeted, but in Norwich it held its own, actually rising to about 500 by early 1936.[58]

The next general election was held in 1935. This time the official Labour Party put up two candidates of their own in Norwich. The local Party appear to have been happy to put up just one official Labour candidate and allow the ILP to be in effect the second Labour candidate: however, the National Executive of the Party would not allow it. There were hopes that Dorothy would stand once more for the ILP: however, she declined for 'personal reasons', no doubt because of Maud's state of health, which had been giving concern for some time: in 1934, the pair had gone on a cruise to Palma, going out on the *Orford* in January and returning on the *Orama* the following month.

Once Dorothy had decided not to stand, Shakespeare was generous in his praise, describing her as 'a local candidate who for her long record of social service is loved by a large number of people'.[59] In her absence, Fenner Brockway, one of the leading lights of the ILP but a man with no Norwich connections, stood. At the nominations for the candidates, Brockway had to reveal a fact that he confessed he kept hidden whenever he could: his first Christian name was Archibald! He put himself forward as 'the only no-war candidate' and echoed Shakespeare's praise of the work that Dorothy had done.

Where the official Labour Party put up candidates against it, the ILP had very little chance of success. Brockway polled only 6,736 votes and had to forfeit his £150 deposit. Dorothy might have done better, but clearly the seat was now beyond the ILP's reach, as she was no doubt fully aware. Nationally, one of the very few ILP people to win a seat was Campbell Stephen: he had lost his seat in 1931 but regained it in the 1935 election even though the official Labour Party put up a candidate against him.

Dorothy's pacifism had come to the fore in 1931. A local Joint Disarmament Campaign Committee was formed in Norwich in June 1931, to campaign prior to the World Disarmament Conference to be held in Geneva in February 1932. Dorothy was one of the speakers in this cause, and held a weekend school to promote it in September 1931. This association with pacifism may also have cost her votes in the election in the following month. The cause was always a minority one: the Committee had hoped to stage a rally in St Andrew's Hall, but had to cancel it through lack of interest. The Conference itself began with high expectations, but fell apart after Adolf Hitler withdrew Germany from both the Conference and the League of Nations in 1933.[60]

Dorothy's name twice appeared in *The Times* as signatory, with other left-wing figures, to letters concerning causes to which she had devoted her life. In February 1935, over 60 prominent people – mainly but not exclusively women – condemned the current practice of giving unemployed women two shillings a week less than men, and 'female young persons' a shilling a week less than their male counterparts. In October 1936, Dorothy, along with 34 others, including Laurence Housman and Vera Brittain, wrote to hope that the Factory Bill about to go before Parliament would lay down a maximum working week for adults, and would regulate hours and working practices for young people. This was to be her last intervention in national politics.

8

Dorothy in local politics
1927–37

On 16 October 1927, Dorothy was adopted as Labour candidate for Wensum ward in the elections for Norwich City Council. She made a typically aggressive speech:

> The Labour Party stood for the Socialisation of all essential services. These should be run primarily on the principle that the first consideration is the well-being of the citizens. Finally, they must remember that there is no real solution of all these problems within the confines of the Capitalist system. It is the failure of Capitalism to solve these problems which condemns it and makes the growth and ultimate triumph of Socialism inevitable.[61]

In the event Dorothy was elected unopposed. She took her new role in politics seriously, and was a very active councillor: her main fields of interest were unemployment and children's welfare. She immediately became a member of several council committees that reflected her social concerns – Health, Pensions and the Care of the Mentally Defective, as it was then called. However, unemployment was her main concern, throughout her council career: she put forward a resolution on the subject as early as March 1928. This urged the Executive and Parks and Gardens Committees to say what schemes of work they were proposing for the unemployed. In September 1930 she proposed that the Minister of Health try, as an experiment, providing milk 'to the children of a particular school in a poor district'. The council was divided, six for and six against: the matter was not taken any further.[62]

Each councillor served a three year term, so Dorothy came up for election again in November 1930. She scored a great individual victory in her ward, trouncing her only opponent, a Conservative, W. G. Hovell, by 976 votes to 366. She joined the new Public Assistance Committee, which had been set up to replace the Board of Guardians: the Government laid down the rates of outdoor relief and provided about 50% of the finance. She also served on the Unemployment Committee. In June 1931 she proposed a stop to the decontrolling of rents, the setting up of Fair Rents Courts to protect tenants and sub-tenants, and also a reduction in rents from 40% above pre-war levels to 20%. The motion was carried.

In December 1932 she urged the Public Assistance Committee that no deduction should be made to any person's relief to pay for any false teeth! The idea was heavily defeated – in fact she was the only councillor to vote for it – and when she brought it up at the Council itself it was again defeated.

Dorothy rarely missed a meeting of the Unemployment Committee, and her work was perhaps her greatest contribution to the city she loved: the committee set up schemes which were intended both to create work for the unemployed and to revolutionise the infrastructure. They included reconstructing roads around the city such as Martineau Lane and Colman Road to create the Outer Ring Road, and the creation of many new parks and playgrounds, such as Eaton Park and Waterloo Park. Other schemes included widening the river, beginning the Riverside Walk and the construction of Earlham Library. Much work was done on Mousehold Heath,

A major programme of parks improvements in the 1920s and 1930s added to the quality of life in Norwich – and provided work for the city's unemployed. This is Eaton Park.

including setting out Norwich aerodrome there. These schemes depended on Government grants. When these were discontinued in 1932, the council decided not to carry on any more work schemes. In March 1933, Dorothy put forward a motion asking the council to rescind this decision: she proposed that the Council should spend £10,840 on unemployment emergency works in the year 1933–34, and, she also proposed that the sum allowed for the feeding of schoolchildren in the year should be raised from £25 to £330. The Council meeting to discuss these proposals was held on 4 April 1933; unfortunately Dorothy could not attend, so they were not raised.[63]

The reason for her absence was a personal one: her mother, Mary, had died suddenly on 3 April, just a month before her eighty-third birthday. The *Eastern Daily Press* paid tribute, pointing out that, although a Liberal, she had acted as hostess when Dorothy brought socialist friends like George Lansbury and James Maxton home: they had found a common compassion, however different their political and religious views. Mary was in fact deeply religious: she read aloud a portion of the Bible every day of her life, even on the morning of the day she died.[64]

Mary's funeral service was at the Silver Road Baptist chapel, followed by burial in the family plot in the Rosary, alongside her husband. Dorothy and her three surviving siblings were present at the funeral: political divisions had had no effect on family unity. Maud was now sufficiently a member of the family to be included among the immediate group of mourners.

Mary's will had been made many years before in 1917, after the death of her son Harry but when her husband was still alive: it appointed George and Christopher as executors. As her husband had predeceased her, everything was to be divided among her children, who would now also benefit under the terms of George's will: the family furniture and plate was divided between the two unmarried sisters, Edith and Dorothy.

In November 1933, it was time for Dorothy to face re-election. As we have seen, she had left the Labour Party and she now stood as a candidate for the ILP. The boundaries of the wards had been changed in 1932, and Wensum ward no longer existed. In 1933 she stood for Westwick ward. The official Labour Party did not run against her, although, according to Dorothy, they had tried to find a candidate: her position within the left wing politics of the city was too strong to be challenged. Her only opponent was a Conservative, A. F. J. Frost. Frost was a builder, so she stressed her concern about housing problems: she knew of a house in Norwich where 29 people were lodging with just one lavatory between them. She attacked the policy of the Public Assistance Committee in the same terms as she had attacked its predecessor twenty years earlier: single men being denied relief and forced into the workhouse where it cost nearly 30 shillings a week to maintain them. She knew cases

Norwich Independent Labour Party letterhead.

where less than five shillings a week was being allowed to feed and clothe a family after the rent had been paid.

This was a good year for the ILP in the city. Dorothy herself had a decisive victory in her ward, winning by 1,226 votes to 622. George Johnson won Catton ward for them, despite being opposed by a candidate from the official Labour party. This was a unique election: it was the only occasion in Norwich politics when the ILP were victorious in a direct fight with an official Labour party candidate. After the election, the Labour Party had a majority on the City Council – but only if the two ILP councillors were included as part of the Labour total. The ILP held the balance of power. Naturally, they held a triumphant meeting at Keir Hardie Hall. Their local president was jubilant: 'from now on the Labour group on the City Council has to toe the line. For the first time they are going to be made to face up to working class policies as they promised they would. From today the ILP in Norwich is going forward'. Dorothy joked that when she arrived at the Hall she thought the revolution had started! The two groups maintained cordial relations, in Norwich at least, and there was even a proposal that there should be a joint committee: however, the national Labour Party would not allow this.[65]

George F. Johnson, stalwart of the Norwich Independent Labour Party.

In December 1933 she announced her intention to put forward a proposal that the Council no longer demand a deposit of ten shillings from tenants taking possession of council houses, and that they abolish their Income Scale, which prevented low wage workers from getting a council house. In the event the motion was actually put forward by her ILP colleague George Johnson and was massively defeated – receiving just two votes in its favour.[66]

In January 1934 a new Unemployment Bill came before Parliament, creating a National Unemployment Board that took over responsibility for the long term unemployed. Dorothy was outraged by the harshness of the new law: she put forward a motion that the City Council 'emphatically condemns' the Bill, and gave eight reasons. Three of the points were typical of Dorothy's thinking:

> *It retains the present inadequate scales of benefit and the Means Test with all its injustices;*
> *It continues the Anomalies Act which has deprived many unemployed persons of their right to benefit;*
> *It attacks Trade Union conditions and wages.*[67]

The motion, which called on the two Norwich MPs to oppose the Bill, was carried, but the Bill became law.

In the November 1934 elections, Alf Nicholls won a second seat in Catton for the ILP, but, like Dorothy, he had been given a free run by the official Labour Party. The new council elected Dorothy's cousin Percy Jewson as Lord Mayor. The two were of different parties – Percy remained true to the family's Liberal traditions – but had some interests in common. One of the mayor's charities involved raising money to buy boots for school children whose parents could not afford them; Dorothy

Dorothy's cousin, Percy Jewson, in mayoral robes in 1934, at the start of his year of office.

contributed ten shillings. Dorothy was present in June 1935 when Jewson formally opened the new playground at Lakenham; rivals and colleagues present included Witard, Henderson and Shakespeare. The park was seen at the time as the final link in the council's campaign to supply recreational facilities in all parts of the city, and had helped provide work: it gave work to 27 unemployed men for fifty weeks. The playground consists of six acres at the top of Long John Hill. The council paid £605 to buy the former gravel pit and tip, and spent a further £3,183 on levelling the site, grassing it and putting in a sandpit. It was intended for 'disorganised games'.[68]

Dorothy and her ILP colleagues formed a small but often rowdy left-wing group on the Council: her cousin who, as Mayor, chaired the meetings must sometimes have found the family connection embarrassing. At the first council meeting at which he presided, in November 1934, the ILP councillors argued with their fellow councillors about the scale of assistance given to the needy, which the Public Assistance Committee recommended should be unchanged from the previous year. Dorothy said it was wrong to say Norwich was generous in its assistance, as Labour councillors regularly claimed. She thought the scales were unfair — £2 a week was given to a married couple with children regardless of how many children they had — nobody could convince her that eight children — or more — could be fed on £2 a week! She and Johnson interrupted other speakers, and, when she rose to speak again, the Mayor had to remind her that she could not speak a second time: to cries of 'Sit down!' she resumed her seat. The motion put forward by the ILP councillors was heavily defeated.

At the December council meeting she returned to the issue saying that the council had responsibilities to the unemployed which it could not shelve: many citizens of Norwich were going to suffer a great decrease in their standard of living. She put forward a motion calling on the two Norwich Members of Parliament to vote against the new scales of relief, and her motion was carried by 22 votes to three. When the debate turned to the work on the new City Hall, which involved pulling down many older buildings, she asked if local unemployed men could do the work: she was told that it would be put out to tender. The meeting was held in difficult circumstances. About fifty local unemployed men had gathered outside the Guildhall: as the councillors left, the men chanted 'WE WANT WORK'.

In March 1935 she succeeded in abolishing the deposit that the Housing Committee required from new council house tenants. She said that tenants on relief could not afford the deposit, and that other local authorities did not require one: her motion was carried. Housing was also on her mind in May when she complained that the Housing Committee had no defined policy as to who to prioritise from the waiting list for new council houses: she quoted a case where a woman and six children living in a one-up one-down house in Silver Road had been refused a house while a nearby couple with no children had been accepted: she conceded the couple had been on the list 'a bit longer'. The members of the Housing Committee naturally defended themselves, claiming that they selected the worst cases on the list.

The ILP received a further boost when Arthur South won Catton ward for them in the November 1935 elections, held during the general election campaign: Dorothy had spoken for him at his adoption meeting. At the age of 22, South (today best known in Norwich for his role as chairman of Norwich City FC in the 1970s), was the youngest councillor in the British Isles. However, once again he had won only because he had been given a free run by the official Labour Party. The ILP now had four seats on the city council: this was to be their high point in city politics.

'The ILP-ers' formed a small but very close band, conscious of their place in the history of Socialism. Henry Cadman, a former full time Labour Party organiser, stood unsuccessfully for the ILP in the 1932 local election at the age of 70. He died in June 1935: Dorothy wrote to his widow, associating Maud in the letter of sympathy: 'We were all so fond of your husband, and he had so much insight and understanding of the Labour movement for which he did so much, that he will be a great loss. Our thoughts are with you – Miss Murray's and mine'.[69]

The working class in Norwich remained loyal to 'our Dorothy' despite her departure from the Labour Party. In July 1936 she was chosen to formally open the club established by the Unemployed Workers' Movement in Norwich. This was in

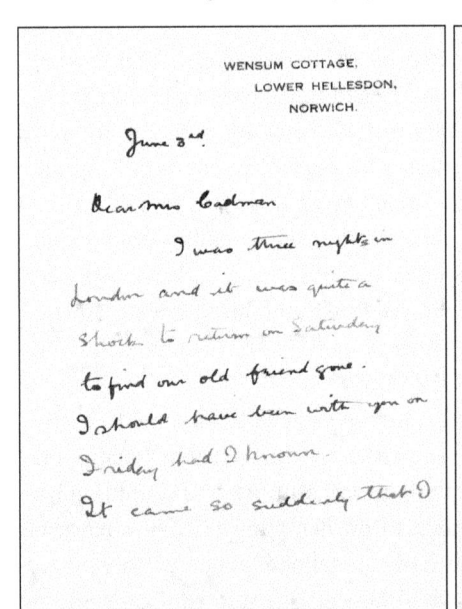

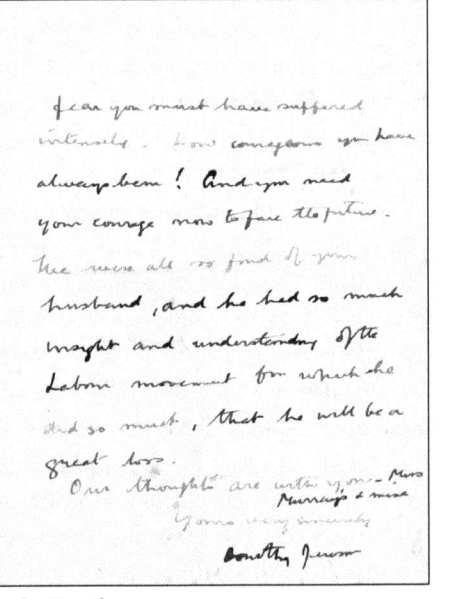

Letter of commiseration by Dorothy, 1935.

Shave's Court, Colegate: it had a gymnasium, reading rooms, a lecture hall – and two full-sized billiard tables. Dorothy congratulated the movement on converting an old factory into a 'fresh and airy' club. She urged the unemployed to use their organisation 'for fighting for human rights – the right to a place in the sun'. She spoke against the new unemployment rules, and was applauded when she said: 'we condemned the old regulations because they meant a big reduction to the unemployed of Norwich. We shall equally condemn these because they mean a big reduction'. In September she moved an amendment to a Housing Committee report on council flats to urge that 'as a general rule, persons with children under ten years of age should not be accommodated in flats': her proposal was defeated.[70]

From October 1936, Dorothy began to draw back from politics at both the national and local level. The cause of this withdrawal was a highly personal one: Maud Murray died in a nursing home at 32 Surrey Street, Norwich, on 9 October 1936; she was 53. Maud was cremated in her home area of London, at Golders Green, on 12 October. She left no will and the administration of her goods – valued at only £315 12s – passed to her father, George, now described as a 'retired confectioner'.

Dorothy was shattered and, most unusually for her, was absent from the council meetings of October 1936. However, she allowed her name to go forward for the November 1936 election – there was no campaign to fight as she was returned unopposed. She attended the first meeting of the new council in November, but then was absent until March 1937, for at least part of the time on the cruise described in the next chapter.

On 31 March the Relief Committee ceased to have responsibility for poor relief, with the Unemployment Board taking over on 1 April. Responsibility for the poor had passed from the local council to the Government: it was the end of an era, and Dorothy must have felt it as such. It was also the cause of a heated debate in the Council Chamber on 16 March, which Dorothy attended. Normally the Council handed out weekly benefits on Monday: as the Government was taking over at the end of the week, the question was whether to give out five days money, or that for the full week. This caused heated argument in the council and the local press, some people arguing that if the Council gave out money for seven days they could be accused of wasting ratepayers' money, and be surcharged or even imprisoned! In the end, the Council voted by 44 votes to four to give out the full week's money: Dorothy, unusually, was in the majority.

Dorothy was absent from the May and June council meetings. In July, she fought for a typical social issue, the provision of a Municipal Dental Clinic in Norwich. One had been set up in Shoreditch, and Dorothy wanted the city to follow this example. Her campaign, again typically, was a failure. The Health Committee voted against the idea by six votes to one on 9 July 1937. On 20 July Dorothy raised the matter at a full council meeting. Her proposal to consider the matter at the next meeting was rejected by 18 votes to 16.

In the event, this was to be the final act in Dorothy's political career. On 20 August 1937 she resigned from the Council; she had not got over Maud's death, and she had lost her will to continue. The *Eastern Daily Press* carried a frank statement: 'the death of the lady who was her close companion . . . at Hellesdon came as a great blow to Miss Jewson.'[71]

The work put in by Dorothy and her colleagues had transformed the infrastructure of the city in the ten years during which she was on the Council: when Waterloo Park was opened in 1933, the city proudly announced it had now had 718 acres of open space, one acre to every 178 of the population. An American wrote to the *Eastern Daily Press* in 1937 after visiting the city for the first time for eight years: 'I was hardly prepared for the transformation I found there. I was impressed by the army of beautiful new houses . . . In the planning and setting out of public parks Norwich has excelled herself'. The present-day citizen can be thankful for what was achieved by the City Council in the 1930s. Dorothy had played an important part in this work. Her personal popularity can be seen in the result of the by-election in Westwick after her resignation: the ILP vote fell by well over half, and the Conservatives took the seat.

The opening of Waterloo Park, Norwich, 29 April 1933. The Lord Mayor, H. N. Holmes, is bowling.

9
Afterwards
1937–64

At the age of 52, Dorothy's life now changed in very many ways. To overcome her distress, she made a voyage to South Africa in the spring of 1937. She travelled back on the *Warwick Castle*; on the cruise, she met Richard Tanner-Smith, a tea merchant and fifteen years her senior. He was an experienced passenger, having been on cruises to both America and Australia with his first wife, Alice, who had died aged sixty in 1934. The ship docked at Southampton on 8 March 1937; soon after her return, their engagement was announced and Dorothy married Tanner-Smith in Lambeth on 12 August 1937: they moved to his home at Goodmayes in Essex. However, Tanner-Smith died in July 1939, less than two years after their marriage.

True to her pacifist principles, Dorothy opposed the war which broke out in September 1939. She was active in the Peace Movement, and she joined the Society of Friends, attending the Ilford meeting during the war.

In 1945, Dorothy married Campbell Stephen, who was still in Parliament as an ILP MP. At the age of 60 it was his first marriage; Dorothy was the same age. This marriage too lasted no more than a couple of years before death intervened: Stephen rejoined the Labour Party only a week before his death in Glasgow in October 1947. His obituary in *The Times* noted that 'he scorned the social graces altogether' but praised the great work he had done for his poorer constituents. A follow-up by fellow-MP Godfrey Nicholson said that although he had appeared 'dour and unaccommodating' he 'had a warm and kindly heart': once touched by an issue he would respond loyally. At this time, Dorothy must have thought once more of Maud, a decade after her death: there was a second grant of probate on

Dorothy's reminiscences in a letter to Fred Henderson — note the reference to Maud Murray.

her estate, the effects now valued at a mere £67 2s. This time Dorothy acted as administrator.

After Stephen's death, Dorothy moved to Orpington and attended Petts Wood meeting of the Friends. She was formally admitted to the Croydon and Southwark meeting on 12 November 1958. Her campaigning days must have seemed far away: when she sent some reminiscences of her union work to Fred Henderson in the 1950s, she began the notes by saying: 'I feel like a ghost who returns to visit [an] old house that had its heyday about 40 years ago'. In 1961, she wrote from her Orpington home to tell the City council that she was leaving them £3,000 for the benefit of old people in Norwich.[72]

In old age, it was time for Dorothy to return. Christopher and his wife Annie were still living at Riverdene: in January 1963 they submitted a plan to extend the house to provide a ground floor flat and maisonette. It took time to get ready: Dorothy made several visits to the city in the spring of 1963, attending the Society of Friends Meeting, and finally moved back to Norwich in September 1963. She was looking forward to the spring in her home city but did not live to see it: she died in the Plantation Nursing Home on Christchurch Road in Norwich on 29 February 1964 at the age of 79. Christopher comforted himself with the thought that had she been still living in Orpington, she might well have lain in her house for days before being discovered. He also found strength in the thought that he and his sister had at least had six happy months together.[73]

Dorothy's parents are buried in the family grave in the Rosary Cemetery, Norwich, which also commemorates her brother Harry, killed at Gaza, and other siblings. However, Dorothy herself is not buried there: like her devoted friend Maud three decades earlier she was cremated. A memorial service was held for her at the Goat Lane Meeting House, followed by cremation at St Faith's, the crematorium just outside Norwich. Although she had only attended for the last few months of her life, the Society, after giving thanks to God for Dorothy's life, raised a sum of money in her memory, which was spent on an 'experimental sand tray' for the Children's Meeting — Dorothy would surely have approved! Her will was proved in July 1964, with her possessions valued at £15,430. The bequest to the City duly arrived: Dorothy left the money for the purpose of promoting the welfare of such old people living in the city or nearby who from poverty, infirmity, ill health or old age are in need of assistance. The money came to the Welfare Committee who decided to invest the capital and use the interest as a general charity fund.

In spite of photographs, it is hard to imagine what Dorothy was actually like. Lesley Hall has pulled out the descriptions of her in an article by Stella Browne: 'tall and slender; walks quietly and with something of an athlete's spring; delicate though resolute chin; brown eyes with straight brows and hair; originally that *brun cendre* which also touches black; now grey at the front and sides giving an eighteenth century *poudree* to her straight clear features; an extremely keen though quiet sense of humour'. Her relative C. B. Jewson (a local historian) recalled her as of middle stature with lively brown eyes and a shock of brown (later grey) hair, and that 'she never lost her youthful enthusiasm'.[74]

Sadly, by the time she died, Dorothy's achievements had largely been forgotten: her obituaries do not do justice to her remarkable career of devoted service to women and to the poor. She had expressed her views on the vital role of the family in her 1926 pamphlet:

> [Mothers and children] had a right to a share of their own in the wealth of the community . . . other services are concerned with the making of things but motherhood with the making of human beings.[75]

Never a mother herself, her whole life and work had been dedicated to helping working women and mothers. Many of the causes for which she fought have come into force now: votes for all adults, the provision of free birth control advice, family allowances, and the abolition of capital punishment. However the struggle for the rights of the poor and oppressed and the campaign for world peace continue. Dorothy deserves to be better remembered both nationally, and, especially, in the city where she did so much good.

The Jewson family grave in the Rosary Cemetery, Norwich.

Notes

1. Her given name was actually Dorothea not Dorothy. From her schooldays onwards, she preferred to call herself Dorothy and I have used this name throughout this book.
2. Quoted in *Norwich High School 1875-1950* (Norwich, 1950).
3. Norfolk Record Office (hereafter NRO), BR 24/56. The cottage was called 'Gavelkind'.
4. The school magazine, *Parvum in Multo*, is held at the present Norwich High School for Girls on Newmarket Road in Norwich, with other relevant documents and photographs, including those in this book showing Dorothy at school. Mr Tom Greenwood kindly allowed me access to the school's archives.
5. NRO, BR 24/56. Written about his sister Constance (at Newnham), it could just as well relate to his equally bright cousins Dorothy and Edith.
6. *Eastern Daily Press* (hereafter EDP) 1 January 1927.
7. EDP 2 April 1974.
8. *The Suffragette* 31 January 1913.
9. *The Suffragette* 24 January 1913.
10. NRO, N/ED 1/54. The logbook mentions only that Miriam Pratt is absent from school. NRO, N/TC 35/7/2 (Staff Committee minutes) gives the details.
11. EDP 31 May 1913.
12. NRO, N/ED 1/54.
13. NRO, N/TC 35/7/2.
14. EDP 15 October 1913.
15. N/TC/35/7/2, 30 September 1913.
16. *Hull Daily Mail* 12 April 1926.
17. NRO, SO 198/5/52/2.
18. NRO, SO 198/5/52/6.

19 C. B. Hawkins, *Norwich: A Social Study* (1910), p. 154.
20 *Carrow Works Magazine* vol. IX no. 2 (January 1916), pp. 72–6.
21 Fenner Brockway, *Inside the Left* (1942), pp. 63–4.
22 NRO, MC HEN 43/130. The quotations in this and succeeding paragraphs are from these notes of reminiscence that Dorothy sent to Fred Henderson, probably at his request, forty years later, as mentioned in the final chapter of this book.
23 *The Times* 23 May 1919; *Aberdeen Journal* 3 June 1919.
24 *Dundee Courier* 26 August 1919.
25 EDP 10 November 1923.
26 Francis Martin, 'Labour and gender' in Duncan Tanner and others (editors), *Labour's First Century* (2000), p. 199.
27 Martin Pugh, *Speak for Britain: A New History of the Labour Party* (2011), p. 201.
28 The details are taken from the *Nottingham Evening Post* 30 November 1933.
29 Pugh, *Speak for Britain*, p. 205; EDP November 1923. The local report of her walk back to Norwich, mentioned later, describes Maud as 'the lady who accompanied her [Dorothy] at meetings during the election' (EDP 31 January 1924).
30 *Dictionary of Labour Biography* volume vii, p. 228; David Howell, *MacDonald's Party* (2002), p. 257.
31 *Dundee Courier* 5 April 1924; *Chelmsford Chronicle* 11 April 1924.
32 Quoted in John Shepherd and Kenneth Laybourn, *Britain's First Labour Government* (2013 edition), p. 80.
33 Dora Russell, *The Tamarisk Tree* (1975), p. 173.
34 *Time and Tide* 15 June 1924.
35 Cited in *Time and Tide* 25 January 1924.
36 *The Times* 5 September 1924; *Dundee Courier* 5 August 1924.
37 EDP 1 January 1927.
38 Baroness Hollis, quoted in the *Eastern Daily Press* 'Weekend' supplement 30 March – 5 April 2013.
39 Stella Browne, *The New Generation;* Martin Pugh, *Women and the Women's Movement in Britain* (2000 edition), p. 197.
40 Baroness Hollis, quoted in the *Eastern Daily Press* 'Weekend' supplement 30 March – 5 April 2013.
41 Sheila Rowbotham, *A New World for Women – Stella Browne: Socialist Feminist* (1977), p. 35; Lesley A. Hall, *The Life and Times of Stella Browne, Feminist and Free Spirit* (2011), p. 145; Pamela Graves, *Labour Women: Women in British Working-class Politics 1918-1939* (1994), p. 90.
42 http://www.unionhistory.info – visited 18 August 2013.
43 EDP 6 July 1926.
44 Dorothy Jewson, *Socialism and the Family: A Plea for Family Endowment*. ILP Publication, not dated.
45 Voters' lists show she was still at Bracondale in October 1927. In May 1929, Dorothy and Maud are listed at the Hellesdon address. In 1929 and 1930, Maud calls herself Maud Millicent Murray; in October 1931 and subsequent years she prefers Maud Macpherson Murray: NRO, C/ERO 1/370–405. For the well, see NRO, BR 332/6g.
46 Howell, *MacDonald's Party*, p. 244; Tony Cliff and Donny Gluckstein, *The Labour Party: A Marxist History* (1988), p. 121.

47 *Oxford Dictionary of National Biography* (2004 edition).
48 EDP 22 May – 1 June 1929.
49 Pugh, *Speak for Britain*, p. 206.
50 Fred Whitemore, *The Labour Party, Municipal Politics and Municipal Elections in Norwich 1903–33* (1986), p. 14; Gibson Cohen, *The Failure of a Dream: The Independent Labour Party from Disaffiliation to World War Two* (2007), p. 23.
51 EDP 12 October 1931.
52 EDP 16 October 1931.
53 EDP 29 October 1931.
54 John Shepherd, *George Lansbury* (2002), p. 289.
55 EDP 29 August 1932.
56 Cliff and Gluckstein, *The Labour Party*, p. 169.
57 Matthew Worley, 'The Red Flag in the City', in Ian Grimwood and others (editors), *Labour in the East* (2009), p. 119.
58 Cohen, *Failure of a Dream*, p. 36.
59 EDP 5 November 1935.
60 NRO, SF 282.
61 EDP 17 October 1927.
62 NRO, N/TC 1/66, 72.
63 NRO, N/TC 1/69, 72.
64 EDP 7 April 1933.
65 EDP 2 November 1933; Cohen, *Failure of a Dream*, p. 151.
66 NRO, N/TC 1/67–72.
67 NRO, N/TC 1/70, 72.
68 EDP 24 June 1935.
69 NRO, SO 198/5/52/4; MC 2959.
70 EDP 14 July 1936.
71 EDP 10 October 1936 and 15 September 1937; NRO, N/HE 11/43.
72 *Oxford Dictionary of National Biography* (2004 edition); *Dictionary of Labour Biography*.
73 NRO, BR 332/6g.
74 Hall, *Life and Times*, p. 156, quoting from Stella Browne's *Medical Critic and Guide* (1925); Joyce Bellamy and L. Saville, *Dictionary of Labour Biography* volume 5 (1979), pp. 119–21, quoting letters written by C. B. Jewson in 1976.
75 Quoted in Sheila Rowbotham, *A Century of Women : The History of Women in Britain and the United States* (1997), p. 129.

Index

Adamson, W. M. 56
adoption 57
Arnell, Dora 12
Arnold (schoolfellow) 11
arson 16, 20–21, 23, 25, 26
Astor, Lady 60

Baldwin, Stanley 48, 55, 61, 65, 66
Barrett, Miss (teacher) 11
Bartels, Olive 25
Barton, E. 11
Beverley, M. 11
Bignold, L. 11
birth control 58–59, 65, 66–67
Bolingbroke, M. 12
Bond, R. H. 37
Bondfield, Margaret
    at International Conference of Labour and Socialist Women 71
    at International Congress of Women 39
    elected MP 54
    leaves ILP 70, 79
    loses seat at 1931 election 79
    ministerial posts 54, 60, 65, 75
    Mrs Pankhurst's view of 42

Bondfield, Margaret *continued*
    President of Federation 45
    on unemployment 52
Brackenbury, Georgina 18–19
Braemar 7
Brailsford, Jane 16
Britannia Pier 26
Brockway, Fenner 37–38, 75, 80–81
Browne, Stella 58, 65, 93
Buntings store 21
Burton, H. 11

Cadman, Henry 88
Cambridge, suffragette activity in 20
Campbell, M. 11
Campbell, J. R. 61
capital punishment 57–58
Cat and Mouse Act 23–24
Chadwick, Robert 57
Cheltenham Ladies' College 12
children, adoption 57
children's allowance 69, 75
Clarkson, Mabel 33
Clynes, J. R. 75
Colegate 8
Colman, Ethel 46, 47

Communism 61–62, 63–64
contraceptive advice 58–59, 65
Copeman, Henry 48
council houses 61, 72, 86–88

Davies, Rhys 66
Davison, Emily 22–23
diet 29–32
disarmament 81

Earlham Library 83–84
Easton, Fred 36
Eaton Chase 20–21
Eaton Park 83
Edwards, George 68
employment laws 70–71
equal pay 60, 81

Fabian Society 14
Fairfax, Griffyth 63, 64, 71
family allowance 69, 75
Fawcett, Millicent 14, 46
Fenn, Anthony 23
Foot, Isaac 57
free trade 61
Friends, Society of 91
Frost, A. E. J. 84

Gadesden, Elizabeth 10, 12
general election
   1923 48–54
   1924 63–64
   1929 71–74
   1931 75–79
   1935 80
General Strike 67–68
Gimingham 10
Girton College 12–13, 14
Giveen, Clara 23
Glasier, Katherine 38
Graham, William 60
Graves, Pamela 67
Grenville, Henrietta 16
Griffith (schoolfellow) 11

Hammond, Florence 42

Hardie, Keir 14, 37–38
Harmer, Miss (WSPU local secretary) 16
Hartland, George 75
Henderson, Fred 23, 24, 87, 92
   wife joins him on council 46
Hill, Edith 28
hockey 11–12
Hollis, Baroness 65
Holmes, H. N. 90
Hotblack, K. 11
housing 29, 61, 65, 72
Hovell, W. G. 83
Howell, David 70
Howlett, Rosa 16
hunger strikes 23
Hurst Park 23

Independent Labour Party
   annual conferences in Norwich 37–39, 70
   anti-war meetings 35, 37
   and birth control advice 67
   membership in Norwich 80, 84–85, 88
   origins 14
   seeks radical reform 56
   splits with Labour Party 75–81
   Women's Group National Advisory Committee 70
International Conference of Labour and Socialist Women (Marseilles, 1925) 71
International Congress of Women (The Hague, 1915) 39
International Socialist Conference (1926) 71

Jacob, E. 11
Jarrold, Mary 9
Jarvis, Kathleen 18, 24
Jarvis, Olive 11, 18
Jewson, C. B. 93
Jewson, Christopher 63, 70
Jewson, Clifford 9
Jewson, Constance 11, 12
Jewson, Daisy 12

Jewson, Dorothy
   and the Board of Guardians 28, 32–34
   and the Cat and Mouse Act 23
   education 9–13
   elected to City Council 82–85
   family background 7–10
   fights parliamentary elections 48–54, 71–74
   first lady advocate 42
   houses she lived in 7, 69–70
   investigates Norwich poverty 28–32
   marriages 91
   as Member of Parliament 55–64
   member of the Society of Friends 91
   moves back to Norwich 92
   moves to London 39
   moves to Orpington 92
   on Norwich City Council 69
   organises Margaret West's defence fund 22
   pacifism 26, 35, 71, 81
   political affiliations 14, 15, 69, 71, 79, 84
   and rail strike 55–56
   school photos 11, 12, 13
   sports 11–12
   Strike Committee 68
   as teacher 15
   thinks Parliament a waste of time 65
   trade union activities 15, 40–45
   visits Russia 61–64
   voyage to South Africa 91
Jewson, Edith 9
Jewson, Ellen Margaret 9
Jewson, Frank 47
Jewson, George (b. 1794) 6
Jewson, George (b. 1848) 6, 47
Jewson, George (Jack) 9
Jewson, Harry 9, 16–19, 22, 25, 42–43
   and the Board of Guardians 32–34
Jewson, Henrietta 14
Jewson, John Christopher 9
Jewson, John William 6
Jewson, John Wilson 6, 8–9
Jewson, Kathleen 9, 12

Jewson, Mary 9, 14, 84
Jewson, Percy 13, 86
Jewson, Richard 63
Jewson, Violet 58
Jewson, William 47
Jewson, William Henry see Jewson, Harry
Jewson's (timber company) 8, 47
Jex, Fred 27–28, 34, 75
Johnson, George F. 80, 85, 86, 87

Keir Hardie Hall 37–38, 80
Kenney, Annie 14

Labour Party
   1926 conference 67
   1929 conference 74–75
   1931 election defeats 79
   first government 55–56
   main opposition party 65
   origins 14
   second government 74
   women members 42, 46, 70
   and World War One 35
Labour Representation Committee 14
Lakenham 87
Lanchester, C. C. 32–33
Lansbury, George 18–19, 45, 68
Law, Arthur Bonar 48
Lawrence, Susan 39, 40, 45–46, 54, 59, 61, 65
   and birth control issue 71
   leaves ILP 79
   loses seat at 1931 election 79
Lee, Jennie 80
legal aid 66
Lightman, Nancy 26
Lowe, A. 34
Lunn, A. C. P. 12

Macarthur, Anne Elizabeth ('Nancy') 41
Macarthur, Mary 39, 41–42, 45, 46
MacDonald, James Ramsay
   against birth control 67
   against war 35, 37
   forms first Labour government 55

INDEX

forms second Labour government 74
Labour Representation Committee 14
resigns from ILP 70
Marcon, W. H. 23
Marion, Kitty 23
Maxton, James 56, 80
Mayo, Winifred 18
miners' strike 67–68
minimum wage rates 41
Mitchell, Kate 27
Moore, William 37
munitions workers 40–41, 45
Murray, Maud
   background 39
   death 89
   election campaigning 52
   journey from London during rail strike 55–56
   shares home with Dorothy 70, 84
   union work 40

National Federation of Women Workers 39, 41
   Albert Hall proclamation 43–45
National Government 75, 79
National Union of General and Municipal Workers 45
National Union of Societies for Equal Citizenship 46, 66
National Union of Teachers 15
National Union of Women's Suffrage Societies (NUWSS) 14
Naylor, Marie 22
Nicholls, Alf 86
Nicholson, Godfrey 91
No More War Committee 71
Norwich
   Agricultural Hall 18–19
   Assembly House 9
   Board of Guardians 32–34, 83
   Bull Close Memorial Hall 26
   Cathedral 25
   Colegate 8
   Eaton Chase 20–21
   general elections 48–54, 63–64, 71–80
   housing 29, 65, 86–88
   Market Place meetings 23–24, 35–36
   parks 82–84, 90
   poverty 27–34
   St Andrew's Hall 17–19
   Thatched Assembly Rooms 18, 37
   Tower House 10, 15
   unemployment 82–84
Norwich Distress Committee 37
Norwich High School for Girls 9–10

Osborne, Daisy 12

Pankhurst, Christabel 14, 16
Pankhurst, Emmeline 14
   in favour of war 42
   speaks in Norwich 17–19
Pankhurst, Sylvia 14, 46
Phillips, Marion 39, 58, 71
   loses seat at 1931 election 79
Poor Law 27–34, 45–46, 53
poverty 27–34
Pratt, Miriam 20, 21–22, 23
protectionist policies 48, 61
Pugh, Martin 65

rail strike 55–56
Read, Ethel 12
Reeves, Annie 17, 34
Roberts, George 35, 43, 48
Roche, Millicent H. 11, 12
Roe, Grace 16
Rosary cemetery 84, 93, 94
Rowntree, B. Seebohm 30
Rump, Emma 27
Russell, Dora 58, 67, 71
Russia 61–64, 63–64

Samuel, Herbert 68
Scott, Kathleen 63
Searle, Alice 27
Shakespeare, Geoffrey 71, 75, 87
Sheepshanks, Mary 39
Smith, Walter
   1923 general election campaign 48–54

Smith, Walter *continued*
   1924 general election 64–65
   1929 general election 71–74
   elected to Board of Guardians 34
   and the general strike 67–69
   leaves ILP 80
   opposes National Government 75
Snowden, Philip 60, 70, 79
Social Democratic Federation 14
South, Arthur 88
Stephen, Campbell 56, 80, 81
   marries Dorothy 91
Stevenson, Len 80
Storr, E. B. 37
strikes 55–56
   see also General Strike
suffragettes 14
   arson 16, 20–21
   poster 2
suffragists 14
Swan, H. D. 48

Tanner-Smith, Richard 91
Taylor, Shephard 18
tennis 11–12
Terrington, Lady 54
Tillett, Jacob Henry 9
Tower House 10, 15, 69
toy-making 36–37
Trades Union Congress, women's branch 52
trades unions
   Dorothy's union activities 15, 40–45
   and political parties 14, 35
   views on child allowances 69, 75
   women in 39–41, 45
Tyson, Leonora 17

Unemployed Workers' Movement 88–89
unemployment 43, 52, 63, 68, 75, 86
   Norwich relief schemes 36–37, 82–84, 87

Unemployment Board 89

wage rates 41, 59–60
Waterloo Park 90
Wells, H. G. 58
Wensum Cottage 70
West Heath School 15
West, Margaret 16, 17, 20, 22–24
Wheatley, John 56, 58, 59
White, George 9
Williams, Ethel 39
Wintringham, Margaret 57
Witard, Agnes 20
Witard, Herbert 23, 70, 80, 87
   anti-war meeting 35–36
Witard, Herbert (younger) 51
women
   discrimination against 52
   equal pay 60, 81
   in the House of Lords 57
   rights over children 57
   suffrage 14, 64, 66
      see also suffragettes
   in trade unions 39–41, 45
   unemployment 43, 52
   voting age 56–57
Women Workers' Charter 44–45
Women's Emergency Corps 37
Women's Labour Party Conferences 46
Women's Social and Political Union (WSPU) 14, 15
   in Cambridge 20, 225
   in Norwich 16–18, 26
Women's Trade Unioin League 39
Workers' Birth Control Group 58–59, 67
workhouses 27, 84
working week 45, 81
World War One 34–43
Wren, Emily 39

Yarmouth 26
Young, Edward Hilton 48, 63

Lightning Source UK Ltd.
Milton Keynes UK
UKHW02f1604290518
323403UK00012B/652/P